T0360645

Globalization and Entrepreneurship in Small Countries

The changeable business environment requires a new business framework and an understanding of the global market trends and the culture that will impact on business. *Globalization and Entrepreneurship in Small Countries* considers important business principles and makes them accessible for entrepreneurs and small business owners. It addresses the role of managers and leaders and management techniques in the context of global strategy of companies, as well as the culture diversity that comes with globalization of organizations. To meet the constantly changing conditions and demands, business must transcend boundaries to get what it needs regardless of where it exists – geographically, organizationally, and functionally.

This book draws together earlier literature on SME development and internationalization from disparate sources into a cohesive body of work, which traces the evolution of our understanding of the topic. It explores just how globalization affects the demand for business and entrepreneurship, and will therefore be of interest to researchers, academics, policymakers, and students in the fields of entrepreneurship, globalization, organizational studies, and SME development in small countries.

Mirjana Radović-Marković is a professor and director of master's studies in Female Entrepreneurship, and a member of the Board of Directors of Akamai University, USA.

Rajko Tomaš is a professor in the Economics Department at the University of Banja Luka, Bosnia and Herzegovina.

Routledge Focus on Business and Management

The fields of business and management have grown exponentially as areas of research and education. This growth presents challenges for readers trying to keep up with the latest important insights. Routledge Focus on Business and Management presents small books on big topics and how they intersect with the world of business research.

Individually, each title in the series provides coverage of a key academic topic, whilst collectively, the series forms a comprehensive collection across the business disciplines.

Persuasion
The Hidden Forces that Influence Negotiations
Jasper Kim

The Neuroscience of Rhetoric in Management
Compassionate Executive Communication
Dirk Remley

Heidegger and Entrepreneurship
A Phenomenological Approach
Håvard Åsvoll

The Politics of Organizational Change
Robert Price

Globalization and Entrepreneurship in Small Countries
Mirjana Radović-Marković and Rajko Tomaš

For more information about this series, please visit: www.routledge.com/Routledge-Focus-on-Business-and-Management/book-series/FBM

Globalization and Entrepreneurship in Small Countries

Mirjana Radović-Marković
and Rajko Tomaš

NEW YORK AND LONDON

First published 2019
by Routledge
52 Vanderbilt Avenue, New York, NY 10017

and by Routledge
2 Park Square, Milton Park, Abingdon, Oxon, OX14 4RN

*Routledge is an imprint of the Taylor & Francis Group, an
informa business*

© 2019 Taylor & Francis

Library of Congress Cataloging-in-Publication Data
A catalog record for this title has been requested

ISBN: 978-0-367-25075-1 (hbk)
ISBN: 978-0-429-28587-5 (ebk)

Typeset in Times New Roman
by codeMantra

Dedicated to our beloved families, for their love, support and sacrifices

Contents

Figures

Tables

Boxes

Preface

The changeable business environment needs a new business framework and understanding the global market trends and the culture that will impact business. The book *Globalization and Entrepreneurship in Small Countries* considers important business principles and makes them accessible for entrepreneurs and small business owners. This book also addresses the role of managers and leaders and ways of managing in the context of global strategy of companies and as well as the culture diversity that comes with globalization of an organization. To meet constantly changing conditions and demands, business has to transcend boundaries to get what it needs regardless of where it exists – geographically, organizationally, and functionally.

The set of three parts provides scholars with a sense of where the field has come from and to where it is heading. The book has the following themes: change of distribution of economic power in conditions of economic globalization; the distinction between "small" and "big" countries; theories of SME internationalization; macroeconomic performance involved small countries such as Serbia and Western Balkan countries; competitiveness of small countries in terms of globalization; attractiveness of Serbia and Western Balkan countries for foreign investments; business and small countries' resilience; creating the culturally diverse organization; managing in a global business environment; gender and diversity in organizations; the future of doing business in multicultural world; and global entrepreneurship.

This book differs from other books as it presents the results of different investigations on entrepreneurship, emerging dimensions in management policy, and position of small countries in terms of globalization. It approaches the subject from a multidisciplinary perspective, covering a broad range of topics. Other books on the subject are almost focused on entrepreneurs and on start-ups in general, but not on understanding the impact of globalization on trends in the demand for business and entrepreneurship in small countries. In this context, the book is designed to encourage the readers to think, consider global business opportunities, and apply their unique ideas into their business. In addition, the outcomes of this study related to entrepreneurship and SME development in small countries, policymakers should see an aspect that must be consolidated within the environment of international globalization. Businesspersons, lecturers, and students in the fields of entrepreneurship and business management are strongly advised to read the book.

Mirjana Radović-Marković and Rajko Tomaš
December 2018

1 The Change in Economic Power Distribution in Conditions of Economic Globalization

Rajko Tomaš

1.1 Natural and Social Global Order

In the last three decades globalization has become the word that is very often used for explaining many phenomena in global trade, economy, politics, demography, ecology, communications, technology, culture, democracy, etc. Its usage for explaining the tendencies in a modern world is sometimes inadequate. It is often attributed the powers it does not have, and it is often used as an explanation of the phenomena that are difficult to prove being caused by it, i.e., in the lack of an adequate scientific interpretation, it becomes a universal cause of a great number of all tendencies in the modern world. Therefore, it is observed as a cause of a great number of phenomena in different spheres of life, while it is also forgotten that it is a synthetized consequence of a technological and economic development. All of these are the reasons for which, before we start the analysis of changes in distribution of economic power in conditions of globalization, we must explain the nature, appearance forms, and range of globalization.

We are the witnesses of divided opinions on globalization in the modern world. Preoccupied with everyday life, local and national development forms, people are often surprised by global tendencies, often perplexed before their implications, and sometimes opposed to the unknown form of internationalization of conditions they live in. Historical overview of the globalization matches the history of trade development, technical progress, transport development, communications progress, colonial conquests, wars, establishment of international standards and institutions. In short, on the example of globalization history we confirm the truthfulness of Protagoras' statement that "man is the measure of all the things; of those that are, that they are and those that are not, that they are not". Planet Earth, by its essence, is a natural global system, and thus globalization is also a natural order of relations on planet Earth. Global natural order on planet Earth is a unity of natural resources, unity of relations and processes that take place among them, as well as free, unlimited action of natural forces and free movement of living beings in the natural environment they live in. Due to the limitation of natural resources on planet Earth, from the aspect of human needs, as well as limited power and contradictions between economic and political interests of human communities, people establish social global order. People have created their communities, established the mechanisms of their functioning, set the limits between them, and set the rules and measures of integration and disintegration of the processes that take place in the organization of humanity. People make decisions on globalization of the world, primarily coming from the relations they have created and that they control. This judgment on globalization is significantly distinguished and it rarely matches the global natural order on planet Earth. People establish the global world according to their own vision, motives, and power, following social laws, often contrasted with natural laws of relations on planet Earth, so global natural order is significantly different than global social order. Human communities are distinguished by economic, political, and military power, so their impact on creation of global social order is different.

1.2 Homogeneity of Human Motivation and Globalization

Among the authors, there is no consent on definition and history of globalization. Thus Frank (1998) claims that forms of globalization have also existed three millennia BC. However, Frank has, obviously, equalized the traces of trade development with the first signs of globalization. Regarding Frank's statement we can ask the following question with reason: whether the trade development determines dynamics, nature, and limits of globalization? The trade is a significant feature of globalization, but it cannot be exclusively reduced to it. People exchange goods when they dispose with its surplus. Commodity exchange does not imply that we live in a global world. As long as there are motives for people to retain the borders between their communities, retaining the right to regulate the life within them by themselves than to set the limits for the mobility of people, goods, ideas, and political movements, the existence of the trade between communities does not mean that they are a part of global order. Global social order can be spoken of only within a context of homogeneous motivation of people throughout planet Earth, which is a rather unreal assumption having in mind the fact that all the resources on Earth are limited and unevenly allocated. Therefore, globalization is determined by the level of the homogenization of human motivation and their communities on planet Earth. It is true that with development of technologies that contribute to labor productivity growth, it occurs that trade is spread in the world, transport is developed, and the methods of communication and exchange of information and ideas are perfected. All of that are the parameters that contribute to homogenization of people's interests in the world which increases the globalization level of relations in the world. The appearance of trade in local and regional proportions is significant for the long-term process of the globalization of trade and economy, but it is not the globalization by itself because it does not take global proportions. According to that, we can speak of globalization only when there are real assumptions for the establishment of homogeneity of the motivation of people in the world. From that aspect, much more realistic is the view of Thomas Friedman (2005) of the globalization history. It distinguishes three periods in globalization history (1.0, 2.0, and 3.0) according to the carrier of global processes and the subject of globalization. In the first period (1492–1800) the carrier of globalization was the countries and the subject of globalization was the natural resources. In the second period (1800–2000) the companies globalized market and labor. The third period of globalization began around 2000 and lasts until today. The carriers of today's globalization are individuals and small groups, and the subject of globalization is the competition for reaching the opportunities that are offered in the market to an individual. Friedman points out that globalization 3.0 is specific by not being typically European or American, which was the case with the previous two. "In globalization 3.0 you are going to see every color of the human rainbow take part" (Friedman, 2005, p. 34). Therefore, according to Friedman, globalization 1.0 strengthened the countries, globalization 2.0 the companies, and globalization 3.0 individuals. However, although it was acceptable that main carriers of globalization process, historically observed, were the countries, companies, and individuals, there is no sufficient evidence that the effects of those carriers on globalization were strictly classified within time frameworks provided by Friedman. For example, the First and Second World War show that in the first half of the 20th century, the countries were the ones that had a great impact on globalization process. During big wars, all the processes specific for a form of globalization have experienced a drop. Establishment of a new order in globalization, as a rule, was always followed by efforts of the states, companies, as well as individuals. Although it is true that in certain periods the countries and companies had a dominant role in spreading the globalization process, we cannot claim that by the establishment of a dominant role of one subject there ceases the impact of the previous dominant subject. Accordingly, modern globalization is a consequence of the synergy of global interests of states, international institutions, companies, and individuals on the market principles. Or, as it was defined by McMichael, "Integration on the basis of a project pursuing market rule on a global scale" (McMichael, 2000, p. xxiii). Historically observed, with the development of technology and labor productivity, there comes the synthesis of the interests of countries, companies, and individuals that they achieve through the globalization process.

1.3 Global Multicultural Entrepreneurial Environment

The fact is that individuals, regardless of the part of the world they live in, today have more of the same information than other people in human past. That is one of the manners of homogenization of people's interests on planet Earth that we have spoken of as a condition of the appearance of global social order. Through homogenization, people feel that the global world is increasingly becoming a condition for the achievement of their motives. Of course, availability of information, simplicity of communication, and low costs of information exchange do not affect only the people's motivation harmonization. They affect the harmonization of the level of education, level of people's competitiveness on the labor market, as well as harmonization of opinion on a series of tendencies in the global world. In addition, this creates the assumptions for the multiplication of the forms of cooperation in research and work in real time without constraints due to geographic remoteness, and very soon, due to language barriers (Friedman, 2005, p. 35). Modern globalization, through the strengthening of individuals, has a strong impact on development of innovations and increase of labor productivity. For that reason, it becomes acceptable for both companies and investors. Globalization, initiated by the motives of individuals and strongly supported by interests of companies and investors, constitutes a multicultural entrepreneurial environment. Potentially, it offers the possibility to unite all the knowledge of the world in a process of development, i.e., so far unrecorded possibility of labor productivity growth. However, we must not forget that globalization that is moved by individuals' motives takes place in the conditions of unharmonized allocation, but still in the conditions of unequal possibilities. Globalization based on motivation of individuals gradually globalizes the labor market and sharpens the competition, which will result in the tendency to harmonize the labor price in the global market. In all cases where this tendency would affect the labor price reduction, we can expect the resistance from the part of employed people, as well as the states. For that reason, the success of globalization moved by individuals' motives will have success in encouragement of development through multicultural entrepreneurial environment to the extent in which the productivity growth effects will improve the economic and social position of the individuals. In addition, we must bear in mind that human motivation for making a decision, as a rule, initiates a range of goals that are not always and exclusively economic goals, and that are variable in time and space. For that reason, the differences in lifestyle, limits, and constraints will exist for a long time in the world, which will maintain, with the reduction tendency, the difference between social and natural global order.

1.4 Paradox of the Competition in Global Economy

Tendencies of relations globalization in the world are not equally acceptable in some parts of the world, in individual markets, and within different social groups. Mostly, there is a compliance regarding the advantages that globalization brings through the reduction of production costs, increase of international exchange, and growth of overall wealth. However, through globalization of economy, the competition also obtains global features, which leads to a gradual convergence of the prices of production factors and profit level. Therefore, by setting new relative relations of prices, i.e., labor productivity, globalization affects the allocation of wealth between the companies, states, regions, social groups, and markets, which affects the change in concentration of economic power. The position of developed and undeveloped countries, then rich and poor people, is not the same in the global world, particularly when the facts testify that as the globalization is more intensive, the rich become relatively richer and the poor even poorer. The contemporary world, at the present globalization level, is not a society of equality, nor a society of equal chances, nor a society of economic freedom.

It is also true that the societies that preceded the present form of globalization also were not any of that, so we cannot claim that modern globalization is retrograde. The modern world does not apply the allocation system that would contribute to globalization leading to a more rational usage of scarce resources, more fair allocation of wealth, reduction of poverty, and provision of the same chances for development and success. The modern global market does not equally allocate the vast effects of market spreading. It awards those that possess property such as financial capital, human capital, or entrepreneurial skills (Birdsall, 2006). Amartya Sen warns that there are good reasons for seeing poverty as a deprivation of basic capabilities, rather than merely as low income (Sen, 1999, p. 20). The global world becomes richer and richer in the economic aspect, but economic and social inequality among people is increased. Of the total growth of global income in the period from 1988 to 2008, 44% was attributed by 5% of the richest people in the world, while 1% of the richest have appropriated almost 20% of the total effect of the income growth (Milanovic, 2016). In the United States, the country that is for almost a century a leader in shaping global movements, from the mid-1980s up to now, the income of the "bottom" 50% of population has not grown, while the income of 1% of the richest has grown by 300% (Piketty, 2014). Milanović (2016) points out that in the United States and other rich countries in recent years there comes a growth in income allocation inequality, which is opposed to Kuznets' hypothesis and which brings it in doubt. The former president of the United States, Barack Obama, in his farewell speech in the UN on September 20, 2016, said: "A world in which one percent of humanity controls as much wealth as the other 99 percent will never be stable" (Obama, 2016). Many young people in the United States today live much worse than their parents did, and the chances for that to change are less and less (Stiglitz, 2015). Analysis of the IMF researchers on inequality in allocation of incomes shows that in the period from 2005 to 2012, the real rate of salary growth was less than labor productivity in a greater number of developed countries (Dabla-Norris, 2015, p. 14), and that the incomes of the middle class in the United States, Great Britain, and Japan either drop or stagnate (Dabla-Norris, 2015, p. 13). Stiglitz warns that the politics have shaped the market in a manner that provides advantages for the rich in relation to the others and that great political power of the rich had an impact on legislation and regulatory role, which provides the self-sustainability of inequality (Stiglitz, 2012).

This image of the world, at the present globalization level, opens many dilemmas on the future of globalization from the aspect of motivation of a great part of humanity to take part in that process. The idea of a free approach to resources, as a base of development, as a method of a rational usage of resources, as a base for establishment of human capital and differentiation of entrepreneurial abilities comes into the sphere of hypocrisy. The belief that the free market, privatization, and deregularization bring benefits to everyone becomes a fallacy for many people. Economic science often observes the phenomena in global economy from the aspect of the principles that are valid in national economy or international trade. However, it is obvious that global economy will become a new big chapter in economic science. Economic freedom, competition, regulation, mobility of people, goods, capital, and knowledge obviously take modified forms in the global world. It is easy to observe that scarcity of resources and goods that can be made with them can easily produce the main reason of all the economic problems that people are faced with. Precisely for that reason, the access to resources must be free and market competition an objective force that performs the rational allocation of resources. Those two facts are often used as arguments for the justification of economic globalization and reforms that are implemented in transition countries. Market selection of manufacturers appears to be, from all known so far, the most efficient method of resource allocation, measured by the proportion of production realized. Competitiveness is based on difference, rather than equality. It brings great advantages to consumers, as well as great efforts to manufacturers. Through it, the selectivity of market is achieved, as well as allocation of resources. However, it was determined a long time ago by Hegel (*The Phenomenology of Spirit*) that each phenomenon abolishes itself. Competition contributes to the efficiency of the usage of resources available, but its nature is such that it abolishes itself, i.e., leads to the establishment of monopoly. Monopoly, in order to maximize its own profit, reduces the production and engagement of resources. Therefore, market selection, based on the principle of efficient usage of resources, leads to the creation of monopoly, i.e., using market power for the achievement of financial goals, rather than efficiency. Economy in the global form is not immune to the same tendencies. Efficiency is used for the acquisition of economic power, and when we master economic power, it becomes crucial in determination of behavior, with all bad consequences for the efficiency of resource usage. Efficiency of market usage of resources is primarily transformed in the domination of economic power over efficiency. In the allocation by prices, market does not distinguish the effects of power from the effects of efficiency. The paradox of competition, verified in national economies, had all the assumptions to be expressed in global economy in its strongest form.

1.5 Disharmony between Motivation According to Consumption and Motivation According to Production

On the other hand, in the domain of consumption, market selection verifies as consumers only those entities that dispose with sufficient amount of money to pay the price of goods. The share in consumption is proportional to the money that the consumer disposes with, rather than his real needs. It is unnecessary to prove that millions of poor people, millions of people on the verge of poverty, and millions of ordinary people do not have enough money to provide for goods, often basic ones, required for the assumption. Therefore, in the modern world in each moment, real needs for the goods aimed for consumption are always higher than the offer of those goods from the part of the seller. Thus, the total intensity of economic motivation toward the consumption of the goods given is higher than the total intensity of economic motivation toward production of the same goods. This tendency corresponds to the conditions of sustainability of the basic model of partial balance: in order to produce goods, the demand for it as a free goods must be higher than its supply as free goods. In present conditions of social relations, from the aspect of freely expressed needs, people would be ready to spend a greater quantity of a goods than they are willing to produce, at any moment. Market, through the prices, solves this disharmony. However, it harmonizes the production scope with the economic power of the consumer, striving for the establishment of the equality of the total monetary value of supply and demand, ignoring real needs of consumers and any aspect of solidarity and humanity.

Market selection does not bring about equality among people. It only verifies and expresses in market prices what each individual can provide in the creation of total production. Through market mechanism, many forms of inequality are caused by the level of economic, social, cultural, and political development of the environment they live in. Market gives partially good answers regarding the manner for producing a maximum quantity of goods with limited resources in the conditions given, but it does not give us any answers about the manner in which we could properly divide the produced amount of goods to all the people within a community. Market promotes the mechanism of distribution according to the economic power of the resource's owner. Dynamically observed, this principle leads to the distribution by which the gap between the rich and the poor is increased. Along with the globalization of economy, the total wealth of humanity increases, but simultaneously there grows the gap between the rich minority and poor majority. Inequality that is created by market allocation and selection is not only a matter of ethics but, more and more, the crucial question of future economic growth. Relative poverty of the majority in a world that becomes richer and richer seriously warns about the fact that global economy becomes a means of an accelerated concentration of wealth in the hands of a few number of people. Concentration of market power in a few hands is equally bad as an excessive regulation (Stiglitz, 2015).

A lot of criticism is addressed to the manner in which the market divides the income between members of a community. History also records unsuccessful attempts of suspending distributive function of the market in the previous century (USSR, China, and other socialist countries). Today in those countries we meet more cruel forms of market functioning than it is the case in developed Western countries. Socialist countries have experienced a great paradox: they have nationalized the property and introduced planning economy on behalf of market inefficiency abolishment, in order to perform the privatization of state capital in the 1990s on behalf of market efficiency introduction. Regardless of the fact that we can address a series of justified criticism to market distribution, still, in order to create greater wealth that will be distributed there must exist the motivation of the producers for doing so. The current market distribution of wealth is not satisfactory in terms of real needs of the population. However, we do not believe that without the increase of wealth production and without motivating those who produce it, it is possible to improve the economic position of the poor. Therefore, elimination of poverty, giving equal chances, solidarity, and humanity are highly valued principles of a modern society. However, they are unrealistic without the motivation for the creation of wealth. Strengthening the motivation for wealth creation will much faster and stronger reduce poverty than the imposing of new rules for distribution in conditions of the unchanged wealth. The latest report of the World Bank (2018) on poverty confirms that in the conditions of world's economy globalization, in addition to inequality growth in distribution between the rich and the poor, there comes poverty reduction. Percentage of population that spends up to 1.90$ on a daily basis (purchasing power parity) was reduced from 35.9%, which was in 1990, to 11.2% in 2015.

1.6 Globalization, Negative Selection, Moral Hazard, and Captured Resources

Competition, while it dominates over the economic power of a company, contributes to the growth of resource usage. It is a good environment for the economic growth but it is rather sensitive to negative selection of market participants and moral hazard. When they act in a maximizing manner, market participants are not motivated to encourage the competition. Efficiency of resource usage will always be less if the companies do not survive on the market exclusively based on efficiency of resource management and if resource owners do not take the total risk of their own economic decisions. In the countries where the rich owners of companies have a strong impact on legislation and other regulations, and thus manage to transfer a part of the risk of their own business decisions onto the country or other market participants, the efficiency of resource usage is reduced. Resources that do not have free access, whose owners are in a way exempt from market selection, i.e., resources that are irrationally used, and the market is unable to improve their usage, are referred to as captured resources. As a free access to resources, competition and market expansion increase the wealth produced, the negative selection and moral hazard that are maintained due to market power, increase the scope of captured resources, reduced the wealth produced, and exert a pressure on distribution based on power. From that aspect, if a global market would be set free from the negative selection and moral hazard, the global world could be much richer and with a less gap between the rich and the poor, i.e., we could reduce the difference between social and natural global order. The growth of gap between the rich minority and poor majority, at the global level, but also within the economies of a great number of countries, creates a resistance to globalization. However, globalization by itself is not the cause of the gap, but the concentration of power in hands of a rich minority which globalization uses for the increase of wealth. Not a single normal man opposes globalization, i.e., international integration that is based on respecting human rights. Resistance comes as a reaction to the functioning of private power system (Chomsky, 2002).

1.7 Neoliberalism and Modern Globalization

Although the ideas of neoliberalism have appeared for the first time in the first half of the 20th century in the papers of Mises (1929), mainly as a criticism of Roosevelt's New Deal and ideas on development of social state in Great Britain, until a serious crisis of Keynesian theory of the 1970s, they were nearly forgotten. As the capital was becoming more and more internationally mobile, Bretton Woods monetary regime was becoming more and more unsustainable (Rodrik, 2011). The fact that Keynesianism has experienced a serious crisis was the reason to examine Keynes's actual contribution to economic theory and economic policy (Pilling, 2014, p. vii), but also to remind that ideas of neoliberalism from the first half of the 20th century could be an alternative Keynesianism (Pilling, 2014, p. 8).

For the exit from economic crisis of the 1970s, large capital needed market deregulation, trade liberalization, tax reduction, limitation of syndicates' role in negotiations on salaries, reduction of the state's role in economy, privatization of the public sector, and reduction of public consumption. The crisis was a good reason and a favorable environment to leave the principles of Keynesianism and implement the ideas of neoliberalism. Since the end of the 1970s, neoliberalism was a dominant doctrine of economic development in the world, supported by large capital and significant international financial institutions such as the International Monetary Fund and World Bank. A new, intensive phase of the globalization of world economy matches the era of neoliberalism. Neoliberalism is based on market regulation of the majority of social relations, on competitiveness as an objective measure for distinguishing success from failure, and on individualism as a starting point of the achievement of social goals. Market should verify each person, whether it is a buyer or seller, rich or poor, and the competition should set aside those who succeeded in the achievement of their goals from those who did not. Therefore, by achieving one's own interests, individuals act on the behalf of the entire society, contributing to the growth of total efficiency of using available resources. Freedom of choice through the market, in conditions of limiting the role of the state, compensates for the choice that state institutions make for people. Although Hayek, one of the creators of the idea of neoliberalism, thought that the state should regulate the market in order to prevent the creation of monopoly, protection of labor conditions, and the natural environment a decisive impact on acceptance of a higher level of deregulation at the end of the 1970s had Milton Friedman, who believed that the role of the state in economy should be stopped whenever it is possible (Friedman, 2002).

After almost 40 years of experience with the application of the ideas of neoliberalism, we can state that it has given a huge contribution to the expansion of global trade, transfer of technology and knowledge, and then efficient provision of public services (Ostry et al., 2016, p. 38). However, economic growth is significantly slower in the neoliberal era than in previous decades (Monbiot, 2016), inequality between countries and between countries grows, and global inequality is much higher than national inequality (Vieira, 2012). Financial globalization has contributed more to instability than it has encouraged investments and growth (Rodrik, 2011). In countries of OECD from the mid-1980s until the end of the first decade of the 21st century, the *Gini coefficient* has growth from 0.29 to 0.316. From 22 countries of OECD, it has grown in 17 countries, including the United States, Great Britain, and Scandinavian countries. In addition, at the same time, income of the 10% of the poorest has grown more slowly than the income of the 10% of the richest people in OECD countries (OECD, 2011). Neoliberal principle of financial openness (capital account liberalization) has enabled aiming of global savings to the most productive investments throughout the world, which suits developing countries to reach money for their own development by borrowing it from abroad, without having to increase national savings. However, opening toward foreign financial flows carries along some serious risks as well (Obstfeld, 1998, p. 10). Foreign direct investments, which include the transfer of technology and knowledge, contribute the long-term growth (Dell'Ariccia et al., 2008, p. 3), while foreign portfolio investments and investments in banks, especially "hot money" and speculative money inflows, do not encourage growth nor provide the division of risk with foreign trade partners (Ostry et al., 2016, p. 39).

Economic inequality between people and states increases more rapidly than economic growth in the neoliberal world. According to many people, global crisis from 2008 speaks of the collapse of neoliberalism, although those to whom it brought great economic advantages and who control the greatest part of global wealth are not willing to confess it.

Crisis after crisis is being caused by a failed ideology (Monbiot, 2016). According to Monbiot, all the crises of a modern world, regardless of the isolation of their form, are catalyzed and deepened by the same coherent philosophy. Neoliberalism has become an ideology that is represented as a neutral natural force, as a direction with no alternative. Ideological dimension of neoliberalism reflects itself in the acceptance of the consequences of competition as a fair outcome of relations in society; dispute of competition as a form of suppressing freedom and spreading irrationality; reduction of taxes and expenses for public needs; privatization of public services; limitation of the range of work and collective negotiations between employers and syndicates as a form of eliminating the disorders in the functioning of labor market; and treatment of inequalities as a reward for the usefulness and a wealth generator that is concentrated in the interest of all people. In the system with such ideological features, we establish a legislation framework which provides reproduction of the relations established. The rich are convinced that their wealth comes from their credits, while the poor blame themselves for their failures, and both believe that they are right (Monbiot, 2016).

Rodrik (2011) claims that main problem of "hyper-globalization", as he calls the goal of neoliberalization, is poor management of global market. Namely, competences of governments are at the national level, while the market is global. In such conditions, if you give big power to governments, you get protectionism and autarky, and if you give a big freedom to the market, you have an unstable global economy (Rodrik, 2011, p. 14).

Stemming from the accumulated wealth in the hands of a relatively small number of people and poverty of the majority, the ideology of neoliberalism is interpreted as a fair outcome of competitiveness and market efficiency. That ideology ignores that accumulation of wealth leads to the concentration of economic power and that eliminates the competition based on neoliberal ideology and promotes moral hazard as ideology of the survival of parasite corporations. Competition, in the first stadium, is accepted as an excuse for the differences between the rich and the poor, but its higher stadium is ignored, when you exit the domain of efficiency and go into domain of power. It is beyond doubt that economic globalization has provided a high level of progress, particularly in developed countries. However, the growth of wealth has not increased economic stability in the world and it has not increased economic freedom of a great part of humanity. Obviously the growth of inequality in the world does not originate only from the differences in efficiency and ability, but also for the great part, from the fact that many companies, banks, and funds are positioned in the global market in such a manner that they obtain a part of their income by the distribution based on market power. That is the thing that feeds the doubt that neoliberalism and globalization phase based on it have used free market as an objective mechanism in evaluation of the efficiency of scarce resources usage to obtain power in the market and distribute wealth through power.

1.8 The Position of Small Countries in the Conditions of Globalization

Opinions on the role and importance of small states in the global world are divided and range from marginalizing their role to highlighting their geostrategic significance for the development of large countries. Smaller countries are often marginalized due to the fact that a small part of the world's population lives in them (e.g. Huntington, 1991; Moore, 1995) and that their sovereignty is limited and thus they are not "real" states (e.g. Vanhanen, 1997). On the other hand, there are studies that highlight the great importance of small countries' experiences in implementing their own economic development strategies (e.g. Frankel, 2012; Skilling, 2012), experiences in the development of democracy and decentralization (Veenendaal & Corbett, 2015), and, in particular, their geostrategic importance for achieving the goals of large countries (Carafano, 2018; Graham et al., 2018).

Regardless of the opinion of small countries and their economic and political power, the fact is that they exist and that "citizens in small countries have the same expectations, aspirations and natural rights as those in the world powers" (Carafano, 2018). According to the classification criteria adopted in this book[1] and the total number of entities for which the IMF manages data on GDP, in 2017 there were 88 large and 138 small countries. In large countries, there were 95.17% of the world's population, and they disposed of 91.75% of the world's GDP. At the same time, in the small countries, lived 4.83% of the world's population with 8.25% of the world's GDP available.

1.8.1 The Benefits of Globalization for Small Countries

Globalization in all its aspects influences the change of inherited social standards and traditional habits of small, but also of large countries. In general, due to the disproportionate economic and political power of large and small countries, greater attention is paid to the changes that occur in small countries, although large countries face major changes in the process of globalization as well. Large countries, because of their own interests, bear the greatest burden of globalization: they initiate global changes; they make key decisions that globalize the world, but also bear the bulk of the costs of globalization and take the greatest burden of its risk. The OECD survey has shown that the growth of foreign trade (trade exposure) of 10% of GDP results in a 4% increase in per capita income (OECD, 2003). Thus, economic globalization is a major global project, a major investment, which brings benefits for improving business worldwide. Small countries participate in global projects. In order to take advantage of the globalization of the economy, they must have a very flexible policy of cooperation with the environment, a policy of adapting the conditions of business and managing their own development.

Globalization brings a number of advantages for the development of small countries. The first, and probably the most important advantage for their development, is to open a relatively large market. The free global market is relatively multiply greater than the supply of individual small countries. This advantage is, to a lesser extent, available to large countries due to higher supply. The advantage of a relatively large global market allows small countries to achieve a significant growth in domestic production, exports and income with relatively small imports of investments (by borrowing abroad). All this affects the growth of employment and consumption. The large markets bring special benefits to small countries located in its vicinity. Another advantage of globalization for small countries is to facilitate access to modern technologies and financial markets. Small countries have limited funds for the development of innovation and modern technologies, although the contribution to innovation by small countries should not be underestimated. The availability of modern technologies, the openness of financial markets, and large markets for goods and services determine the very progressive environment for the development of small countries. They are offered the opportunity to use economies of scale and specialization in production on the basis of comparative advantages. The third advantage for small countries comes from the effects of competition on the global market. Competition restricts monopoly margins, reduces prices of goods and services, and contributes to their stability. Globalization has revealed many competitive advantages of small and underdeveloped countries and enabled them to develop and reduce poverty. The fourth advantage is the establishment of geographical price equivalence, the structure of consumption, the elimination of surpluses of supply or surplus of demand in the partial markets, and the contribution to the economic and social stability of the society. Freedom of movement of goods, labor, capital, and ideas allows individual countries to solve easier a number of structural disorders. For example, by joining the European Union (EU), former socialist countries have reduced unemployment by economic migration, improved the structure of consumer goods, discovered their competitive advantages in certain production, and thus attracted investors, which accelerated their economic development.

We have only highlighted here general advantages for small countries. For each individual country, a specific system of advantages brought about by globalization can be set up. Depending on the geographical situation, the proximity of large developed countries, and large markets, small countries can achieve great advantages in the development of transport, infrastructure, security, culture, etc. Small countries should base their development strategies on the system of advantages brought about by globalization. In the conditions of aspiration of large countries to global domination, the geostrategic and geopolitical position of small countries is gaining momentum in the modern phase of globalization, which is also reflected in support of their economic growth. "A small state in the right place can be very important to a big power" (Carafano, 2018).

The truth is, globalization is not a process that only expands prosperity. It also has its own costs and risks, for big and small countries. Globalization leads to the spread of noncompliance, to an increase in ecological costs, to rising energy prices, to rising food prices, to economic migration, and the like. However, for most of these tendencies, globalization itself should not be blamed. What we verify as negative consequences of globalization is most often the consequences of inefficient management of resources, processes, and institutions in the conditions of globalization.

1.8.2 The Countries of the Western Balkans in the Process of Globalization

The EU under the Western Balkans implies countries in the Balkan Peninsula that have not yet become members of the Union. The Western Balkans includes the territory of six small countries: Albania, Bosnia and Herzegovina, Montenegro, Kosovo*,[2] Macedonia, and Serbia. It is a region of 208 thousand km^2 (roughly like Belarus), with about 18 million inhabitants (less than in Romania), and generates less than 1% of the EU's total GDP (0.55% in 2016). GDP per capita is around 4,500 euros, which is only about one-third of the average GDP per capita in the EU. This is one of the poorest regions in Europe that is characterized by high unemployment, a low level of foreign direct investment, a large degree of economic migration, especially of young people, depopulation and average aging of the population, nontransparent public money spending, a weak rule of law, a high degree of corruption, and a gray economy. The two biggest countries in the Western Balkans, Serbia and Bosnia and Herzegovina, have not yet reached the 1990 GDP level in prices (only reached 85%), although all transition countries have emerged from the transitional recession in the first five years after the start of the transition (Tomaš, 2013b). When it comes to the Western Balkans, one should not forget that historical memory here is much longer and that the much greater influence of the past on the present and the future is greater than in other parts of the world.

Although it is a region that has been abandoned by its inhabitants in search for a better life, it is often the subject of political disagreements among large countries. The Western Balkans has found itself on the path of interests of the EU, the United States, Russia, China, and, lately, Turkey. More and more often Russia's return to the Balkans and the search for the "door openers" for the EU and NATO (LSE, 2015) is increasingly talked about, the inability of Russia and Turkey to offer an alternative to the integration of the Western Balkans into the EU (Suedosteuropa-Gesellschaft; SWP, 2014), to the warning that: "The Balkans can easily become one of the chessboards where the big power game can be played" (Mogherini, 2017). So, although poor, the Western Balkans is in the center of the interests of the most powerful powers of the world. It is the evidence that small countries in the process of globalization can be of great significance, despite low economic power. The development of events shows that this is not a very happy circumstance for the Western Balkans. Although it is a strategically important region to the most powerful forces of the world, the Western Balkans is poor, underdeveloped, and unstable. Why is the Western Balkans so important?

There are two main reasons for the interest of the great powers of the Western Balkans:

1   The EU, the United States, and Russia regard the Western Balkans as an important factor in their security and the protection of wider interests.

2   China and Turkey in the Western Balkans see a strategic region to bring them closer to the EU market.

All the countries of the Western Balkans are unambiguously committed to full membership in the EU. They are located in an environment of EU member states with whom they share historical and cultural heritage and with which they realize significant economic cooperation. True, relations with neighbors are not the virtues of this region, but European integrations are a good way to change that and become a factor of regional development. Also, the EU is firmly committed to the European perspective of the Western Balkans because it is in the political, security, and economic interests of the Union itself (European Commission, 2018).

The United States, Russia, China, and Turkey are aware of the inevitable European future of the Western Balkans. However, they are trying to incorporate in their European integration process their interests that these countries will bring into the EU, thus enabling them easier access to the EU market and easier communication with the EU in a number of strategic areas of development and regional security.

The United States is aware that the Western Balkans is a question of the vulnerability of Europe and its security, and Europe's vulnerability affects the national interests of national security (Graham et al., 2018).

Russia has significant cultural and historical ties with the Western Balkans, especially with Serbia and Montenegro. After Montenegro's accession to NATO, the country that had very strong cultural, historical, and economic ties with Russia, even stronger than Serbia, it became clear that the progress of the Western Balkan countries toward full membership in the EU and NATO narrowed the space for the influence of the countries that are outside of this integration. For Russia, it is undisputable that the future of the Western Balkan countries is in the EU. However, Russia does not like linking EU membership with NATO membership. This unambiguously confirms Russia's view of the Western Balkans as a region of special importance for the security of Russia and its interests. Serbia's military neutrality approach is in favor of Russia and it seeks to strengthen Serbia's ability to preserve its commitment.

Turkey supports the European perspective of the Western Balkans. In the process of integration of these countries into the EU, it seeks to use its historical links in the Balkans to consolidate its economic position on the EU market, since in recent years it itself has departed from the EU and its own integration path.

In the past, China did not have significant historical, cultural, and economic ties with the countries of the Western Balkans. Its interest in this region has grown after the idea of the New Silk Road being promoted in 2013. This global Chinese project consists of two components: The Economic Belt of the Silk Road and the Maritime Silk Road of the 21st century and is financially supported by the Asian International Infrastructure Bank (AIIB). Although Western countries had reservations about this Chinese initiative, many EU and NATO members are cofounders and have governors in the AIIB (e.g. Germany, France, Italy, Spain, the United Kingdom, and others). No Western Balkan country is the founder of the AIIB. While the EU is dealing with its own internal contradictions, the economic crisis in individual members and the Brexit, China offers the Western Balkans what they lack most: investments. Although the countries of the Western Balkans are not always fully aware of the long-term implications of these investments in terms of their own macroeconomic stability, they accept them because they contribute to addressing significant development problems without complicated procedures (e.g., the highway in Montenegro, bridge in Belgrade), but they are not conditioned by major reform efforts. Recalling the growing presence of Chinese investments in the Western Balkans, European Commissioner Johannes Hahn noticed in mid-last year that China could turn the region into a "Trojan horse", etc. because we are "witnessing one pattern of China's behavior, "a business model" offering attractive or less attractive loans. If you cannot repay them, then it turns into Chinese capital" (Heath & Gray, 2018).

1.8.2.1 Economic Dependence of the Western Balkans

An analysis of the structure of goods turnover in the countries of the Western Balkans (see Table A.1) reveals a different picture than it could have been formed through a previous analysis of a network of geostrategic and political interests.

In 2017, the most important foreign trade partner to all the countries of the Western Balkans were EU member states. It was similar in previous years. On average, 58.9% of exports and 56% of imports of goods took place with the EU countries. The following by relative importance is intraregional trade. The countries of the Western Balkans mutually export 25.3% of the total export of goods and import 15.8%. Thus, 84.2% of the total export value and 71.8% of the value of the import of goods is realized with the EU countries and within the Western Balkans. The largest foreign trade partners of Serbia are in the EU (64% of the value of exports and 60 of the value of imports), and among them are Italy (12.8% of the value of exports and 10.1% of the value of imports) and Germany (12.2% of the value of exports and 12.6% of the import value). In the Western Balkans, its biggest partner is Bosnia and Herzegovina (7.8% of the value of exports and 2.7% of the value of imports). The data unambiguously confirm the full trade dependence of the Western Balkan countries on the EU and on trade with each other. The smallest countries in the Western Balkans, Montenegro, and Kosovo have relatively higher exports to the neighboring countries of the Western Balkans than to EU countries.

The countries of the Western Balkans export to Russia only 1.5% of the total exports of goods, and they import 2.8%. Of this, the largest exporter and the largest importer from Russia is Serbia with 5.7% of the value of its own exports and 7.3% of its own imports. China and Turkey are the largest foreign trade partners of the Western Balkans than Russia. China accounts for 1.4% of the value of exports and 7.9% of the value of imports, while Turkey exports 2.7% and imports 5.6% of the value of goods from Turkey.

At the same time, in 2017 China was the EU's largest import partner (about 20% of total imports outside the EU), and Russia was the EU's third largest import partner (7.8% of total imports outside the EU). On the export side, China was the EU's second largest partner (about 11% of total exports outside the EU), Russia the fourth (4.6% of total exports outside the EU), and Turkey the EU's fifth largest partner (about 4.5% of total exports outside the EU) (Eurostat, 2018).

High level of foreign trade concentration confirms the calculation of the Hirschman regional trade concentration index (Mikic & Gilbert, 2007),[3] which we conducted for the countries of the Western Balkans based on data on their foreign trade in 2017. The average value of the index was 0.65, which indicates a relatively high concentration of exports to a small number of markets. The highest value of the index has Macedonia (0.82), followed by Albania (0.79), Bosnia and Herzegovina (0.73), Serbia (0.68), Kosovo (0.59), and the smallest Montenegro (0.56). This high value of Hirschman's index explains the high degree of dependence of exports on a small number of markets and the high degree of influence of changes in the EU on economic trends in the Western Balkans.

The Economist researchers, using a regression analysis, found that trade in the Western Balkans, with the exception of Serbia, was seriously under potential opportunities. Current exports to the Western Balkans as a whole represent only 62.9% of potential exports, while for Serbia the value is 90.8% (The Economist, 2018). *The Economist* sees the cause of such a positive trend in Serbia in a strong export growth that is a consequence of the growth of foreign direct investment and the flexible exchange rate of the Serbian dinar. All countries of the Western Balkans, except for Serbia and Macedonia, have overvalued currencies (The Economist, 2018). Recall that Montenegro and Kosovo use the euro even though they are not members of the Eurozone, while Bosnia and Herzegovina have a Currency Board with a fixed exchange rate of domestic currency against the euro.

The countries of the Western Balkans are similar in terms of the structure by consumption and the size of GDP per capita, that is, they are much more similar to each other than with the EU countries, especially to the developed one. Therefore, it would be logical to have a higher level of exchanges, then develop specialization in production (reduce diversification of production) and increase the diversification of exports. However, the level of mutual trade is relatively low and slower than trade with EU countries. For example, Macedonia exports 6.9 times more in the EU than in the countries of the Western Balkans, Albania 5.2 times, BIH 4.4 times, and Serbia 3.2 times. The impression is that the countries of the Western Balkans seek to bring their economies closer to the EU, considering that they will thus fulfill the conditions for full EU membership.

Given that the geographical structure of imports and exports of a country has been shaped for decades, the presented analysis alleviates many of the sophisticated political and media ratings of the Russian, Chinese or Turkish invasion of the Western Balkans. However, the analysis, in truth, in a mild form, reveals that the Western Balkans is no longer ready, as it was at the time of communism, to wait for the promised "brighter future" this time in the EU, while European countries trade more intensively with Russia, China, and Turkey than the countries of the Western Balkans.

1.8.2.2 Economic Perspective of the Western Balkans

The Western Balkans, one of the poorest regions, has found itself at the crossroads of interests of the EU, the United States, Russia, China, and Turkey. Perhaps that is why it is poor too. As a poor region, with a severe historical heritage, it is suitable for spreading dissension, disunity and political manipulation. In such an environment, any assumption of responsibility for the future of the Western Balkans carries a great risk. For this reason, none of the interested countries are involved in taking responsibility for its future. Everyone is in some kind of expectation that the solution appears by itself. The European Strategy for the Western Balkans (European Commission, 2018) so far is a unique document that makes it clear that the Western Balkans is an interest sphere of the EU and that its future lies with the Union. By adopting the Strategy, the EU has told everyone that the future of this region must also be discussed with the Union. On the other hand, the countries of the Western Balkans have long revealed their intentions to become members of the EU. The countries of the Western Balkans measure success in the transition and the effects of globalization by the degree of closeness to the EU. The area for the EU in the Western Balkans is still much larger than the area for Russia, China, or Turkey. The implementation of the Strategy gives the opportunity for the Western Balkans to end their contradictions and to integrate the intentions of the EU and the Western Balkan countries into a unified program of a new future. However, this is an opportunity for the EU to reconsider its current policy towards the countries of the Western Balkans. It has the opportunity to emerge as a winner in one of the most fiercely geopolitical and geostrategic games and to strengthen its global influence. Unfortunately, over the past decades, the EU has not seen in the Western Balkans what others have seen. It insisted superiorly on the implementation of its standards, often neglecting and ignoring the real needs of people in the Western Balkans and sticking to one side in the Balkan misunderstandings. It is therefore no wonder that China, Russia, and Turkey have received some space to realize their interests. The space was relatively open to the EU for a long time, but not everything that people expected and what was needed was done. In addition to the special strategy for the Western Balkans, the EU must also have a specific policy for implementing this strategy. The Union is trying to change the Western Balkans with its directives, to make the smooth Europeans out of the Balkan people, and then to accept them into Europe, while China changes the Western Balkans by investments and by gaining their trust. These two approaches are different in the eyes of ordinary people. From the fact that the Western Balkans lost some of their trust, the EU should learn a lot and adjust its policy. Weak China and Russia are no longer its rivals for the Western Balkans. The Western Balkans is still waiting for Europe. It is time for the EU to free itself of prejudices about the Western Balkans and to accept the Balkans as equal to themselves and to help them manage in the Union. Citizens of the Balkans would be pleased to accept new jobs opened in their countries by European investors, that European products of the same quality as Union's are on the market, that their interest rate on loans raised in EU banks is the same as for citizens of the Union, that they do not pay tuition fees for tuition of children in European universities several times higher than citizens of the Union, and the like.

1.9 Hypothesis of the Research

Through our research we want to verify the accuracy of the tendencies observed in the current phase of globalization of the world economy. Although the total economic wealth of the world was increased during the last phase of globalization, the gap between the rich and the poor was increased; although the market freedom was used as the main method of wealth increase, economic freedom of a great part of humanity was not increased. It is clear that the doctrine of a free market and weakened roles if the state in the last phase of globalization have not managed to absorb all the resources and valorize their prices at the satisfaction of their owners. In the conditions of a relatively big differences in prices of production factors, particularly in potentially big markets, trade liberalization, elimination of barriers for investing in different sectors, and privatization of public companies have initiated global movements of capital towards higher profits. The aim of this movement was not the establishment of equality, harmonization of development, or elimination of poverty. The main goal was and remained a higher profit and higher security of capital placements of the companies to whom the national markets have become small for development. Trade expansion, technology transfer, increase of labor productivity, poverty reduction, expansion of t availability of public goods and services, economic and social development were often the gains that occur along the way in the process of achieving main goal of the companies. However, regardless of that, the last phase of globalization, which still lasts, through the achievement of own goals and casual gains, significantly affects the change in distribution of economic power in the world. Transfer of capital, technology, and knowledge from developed to less developed countries, than the increase of exchange, productivity, employment, consumption, and efficiency of using the resources in less developed countries leads to the increase of their relative economic power. Therefore, although the current globalization process increases the inequality between the rich and the poor, its expansion causes changes in the distribution of economic power in the world. Although globalization leads to economic growth in countries of developing market, it does not establish economic equality, but increases inequality because countries with growing markets reproduce, especially in distribution, relations that are imposed by investors motivated by maximizing the profits. Globalization expands the inequality between the rich and the poor although the distribution of economic power in the world changes. In the regions of the world with a lower level of inequality under the impact of globalization, there comes to inequality increase. Further development of globalization will lead to a change in distribution of economic power in the world, but it won't eliminate inequality or stop the expansion of the gap between the rich and the poor as long as globalization implies unequal conditions and freedom of global mobility of different production factors.

IMF published a study in 2013 on macroeconomic issues of small countries in which there are described the characteristics of small countries that have a decisive effect on their economic and social development (International Monetary Fund, 2013). Due to the absence of the effects of the economy of scope, small countries are faced with relatively high fixed costs in the public and private sector, then with a relatively higher fixed costs of accessing financial and commodity markets, and then high sensitivity to the costs of natural disasters (International Monetary Fund, 2013, p. 9). Such characteristics of small countries have direct consequences to the level of their competitiveness on the global market. When being compared to big countries, small countries have a relatively higher public consumption, limited possibilities for production diversification, limited contribution of labor market to productivity growth, and more expensive and harder approach to investments (International Monetary Fund, 2013, p. 10). In addition to mutual macroeconomic characteristics, the position of all small countries in the world is not the same. Some of them are included in regional economic integrations (for example, small countries of EU), the others are located in the vicinity of big markets, etc. Accordingly, convergence level of economic systems under the impact of globalization is different in small countries. Convergence of economic systems of member countries within the EU has the aim to eliminate or reduce bad impacts on development that originate from the size of a country. Researchers from LSE have determined that in the EU there originate the greatest effects on development due to the trade increase and establishment of a coherent structure of the EU (LSE Enterprise, 2011). As opposed to that, Frankel and Romer (1999), by analyzing global tendencies, have reached the conclusion that correlation analysis cannot confirm the interdependence between trade and income. This fact throws doubt on one of the main assumptions of neoliberalism according to which global trade liberalization will bring benefits to everybody. However, in addition to a series of contradictions, in today's global economy, the greatest economic wealth recorded so far by human history is created. This wealth can be the basis for the creation of a more just and liberal global world. For that reason, today's phase of globalization, in which the wealth produced is increased and inequalities are being deepened, is observed as an unavoidable transient phase that should create a material basis for the new global order. A constituent part of that process is the change in distribution of economic power in the world.

According to the abovementioned tendencies and dilemmas, we will set a main hypothesis of the study:

H0: In a current phase of world economy globalization and, in addition to the increase in the inequality of income distribution and growth of the gap between the rich and the poor, there comes to the change in distribution of relative economic power in the world in favor of the countries of emerging and developing markets.

Globalization has its own reflections on the position of small countries as well, which will be described with more details through the testing of auxiliary hypothesis:

H1: By the expansion of globalization there also grows the relative economic power of small countries in global proportions.

Liberalization of global trade should have a positive impact on the reduction of bad effects of the economy of scope of small countries and strengthening of their economic power. It is not only the economy of scope that affects economic position of small countries in the world. Although they are specific for a series of common macroeconomic features, their economic positions are different. A great impact to economic power of small countries have regional economic integrations that they approach and the vicinity of big markets. Having in mind that the size of a country is a set thing, then that based on it we cannot change economic power, we will pay special attention to the inclusion of small countries into wider economic integrations as a manner of changing economic power under the impact of effects of the economy of scope within a wider market. Our example will be small countries within EU.

1.10 Method of the Analysis

1.10.1 Distinguishing "Small" from "Big" Countries

Among the economists, as well as lawyers and politicians, there is no total agreement regarding the meaning of the term "small country." Attributing greater or smaller significance to one of the criteria of classifying the countries into "big" and "small" (size of the territory, population, development level), the same country can simultaneously be differently classified. The World Bank for small countries, as a criterion for accessing its program of engagement in small countries, defines the population less than 1.5 million. Although among small countries there are great differences, the World Bank finds that they have a few problems in common, with a strong impact on development possibilities: limited institutional capacities, high sensitivity to economic and natural shocks, and inability of using the economy of scope (World Bank; Independent Evaluation Group (IEG), 2016). In addition, IMF and Commonwealth classify their members with less than 1.5 million people as small countries (Commonwealth Advisory Group, 1997; International Monetary Fund, 2017a). The similarity of development issues of small countries does not stop at the limit of 1.5 million people, so the approach to different programs of international support to development is rather flexible. Due to disharmony regarding the criteria of distinguishing "small" and "big" countries, there are many terms in literature such as "micro countries," "giant countries," and "embedded countries" (Laurent, 2008, pp. 30–32).

There is a relatively big number of countries in the world that dispose with respectable institutional capacities, have a significant power to amortize natural and economic shocks, and use the economy of scope rather well and, therefore, they are not "small countries" in the aspect of the definition of the World Bank, and also they are not the most powerful economic and political forces of the world and they do not have a decisive impact on economic, political, geostrategic, and technological movements in the world.

As such, they are significant for regional and overall development. Their position in the global economy fits into the classification of "small countries" that was set 60 years ago by Kuznets (1957).[4] According to his argumentation, all the countries that have less than 10 million people can be considered "small countries." Fifty years later, Laurent has analyzed the popularity of the issue of economic consequences of the size of population that were crucial for Kuznets' conclusion (Laurent, 2008). Although in the meantime, the environment has significantly changed, we reached the conclusion that most arguments of Kuznets on differences between "small" and "big" countries have endured the test of time. Small open countries have managed to overcome "penalties of smallness" due to globalization and the fact that big countries rely on development of the economy of scope in order to provide endogenous national growth (Laurent, 2008, p. 3). In addition, Laurent warns that in the global world we could create the impression that all the countries have become small, so there are no economic consequences of the size of the country (Laurent, 2008, p. 35). On the contrary, size of a country has a great impact on the selection of growth strategy and it will remain so as long as there are countries of different sizes.

Without entering a wider analysis of similarities and differences in behavior of big and small countries, and a more detailed evaluation of the verification of Kuznets' criteria of defining small country, in our analysis we will assume that 10 million people is the border between "small" and "big" countries.

1.10.2 Data and Range

In order to confirm or reject our hypothesis, we will use the data of IMF (International Monetary Fund, 2017b) on GDP of small and big countries in the period 1980–2017. The analysis included 226 countries and entities, for which the IMF records the data on GDP, among which, according to Kuznets' criterion, there are 138 small and 88 big countries. For all the countries, GDP is expressed in current prices in dollars by the current exchange rate. The sum of GDP for all the 226 countries is observed as a whole in which we track the changes in relative concentration of economic power by the countries and by the most important economic regions. For the classification of countries into "small" and "big", we used population in countries in 2017 from the review published by (Worldometers, 2017).

1.10.3 Measurement of a Relative Concentration of Economic Power

1.10.3.1 Description of the Problem

The existing manner of the allocation of global GDP to the countries does not meet any of the criteria of equality (according to the citizen, unit of land's surface, unit of production costs, unit of capital, labor productivity, etc.). Governing manner of distribution of annual GDP in the world implies the inequality of distribution and thus, according to that, the inequality of relative economic power of countries. It means that modern global world functions under the impact of unequal economic power of countries.

Does the inequality of economic power of the countries equals the inequality of the distribution of the world GDP? The distribution of current GDP in the world is the reflection of the current state on particular markets. Economically stronger countries, through trade liberalization, create conditions for the development of the economy of scope in the countries that are present in their markets. Without the economic power of "big" countries, "small" countries, as well as other "big" partner countries, could not use the effects of the economy of scope in the extent in which it is used. Therefore, "big" countries at the global market create greater economic effects that those that are verified in their participation in GDP distribution. For the sake of illustration, we assume that one "big" country, which takes part in international exchange, for some reason entirely disappears from the global market (for example, in the mildest form, it is completely closed towards the rest of the world). This "disappearance" would cause a greater effect in the rest of global economy than the very loss of GDP of that country. A part of resources that the country disposes with would be excluded from the global resource market, world wealth would be reduced and all the people who planned to sell or buy goods in its market would be deprived of such a possibility, which would result in the consequences for the economy of scope and reduction of the GDP of countries in the rest of the world. This drop in economic activity of the rest of the world is the effect that by their existence and functioning within global market there has been created an assumed "disappeared" big country above the GDP amount which was statistically registered in it. Therefore, the total economic power of one country in the global market was defined by the sum of its GDP and effects that its functioning creates for the other economies in the global market. As the GDP of one country is higher, its total economic power is higher and its contribution to the economic power of global economy is also higher. It is usual, although it is not entirely justified, that inequality of the distribution of economic features is measured in the same manner as the inequality of natural features. For example, the share in distribution of the global GDP of 20% is nominally the same as 20% of the concentration of sulfuric acid in a solution, but it does not have the same meaning. The country whose annual GDP is 20% of the total global GDP has a relatively higher impact on the creation of the total economic power in the world, while 20% of sulfuric acid in the solution has the same meaning at any time and any place.

If the sum of the GDP of all the countries in the world for one year, methodologically expressed in the same way, is observed as a whole, we can verify their unequal economic power through the unequal distribution between the countries. By a higher relative concentration of the "world" GDP on the territory of one country, there grows its total impact on all the relations in the worlds, not only economic ones. If the distribution of GDP by countries would be equalized, there would also exist the tendency to equalize the economic power of the countries. However, there are no realistic possibilities for an equal distribution of GDP between the countries on the global market. Economic globalization implies bringing different countries to the same business environment and, according to their economic power, verification of differences between them. In our analysis we will tend to measure the extent in which a relative economic power of countries deviates from their relative share in the distribution of the total GDP. The world will be observed as one community whose GDP is equal to the sum of individual GDPs of all the countries analyzed. Therefore, we will start from the two assumptions:

1 If there is the equality of GDP distribution to the community members, economic power of all the members is the same, which means that their individual impact on overall relations in the community is entirely equalized and, as opposed to that,

2 If the distribution of GDP on the members of the community is uneven, their economic power is different and thus their impact on relations in the community so different.

1.10.3.2 Model

Due to the simplification of the analysis, we will assume that the analyzed community X consists of the subjects A and B which have the same formal-legal status in the community, but simultaneously have a different relative share in the value of some common phenomena k. With k_A we will label the share of the subject A and with k_B the share of the subject B in the value of common phenomena k, where $k_A > k_B$. Values of the phenomena k for the community X is:

$$k_X = k_A + k_B,\tag{1.1}$$

If (1) is divided by k_X, we obtain:

$$1 = \frac{k_A}{k_X} + \frac{k_B}{k_X} \text{ or }\tag{1.2}$$

$$s_A + s_B = 1,\tag{1.3}$$

where $s_A = \dfrac{k_A}{k_X}$ and $s_B = \dfrac{k_B}{k_X}$ are the rates of the share of subjects A and B in the distribution, i.e. creation of value k, where $s_A > s_B$.

The subjects A and B, owing to their activity, create the value of the phenomena k. Therefore, the subject A, because $k_A > k_B$, has a relatively greater significance for its creation. Thus, all the members of the community X, who are in some form dependent from the phenomena k, will be relatively more dependent from the subject A. All those forms of dependence of the community X from the subject A regarding the phenomenon k represent its real economic power and not only its contribution to the creation of k_A. How can we measure this power? In the lack of a more adequate method, we have suggested the *index of the relative concentration of power* – IRC which was obtained by modifying Hirschman-Herfindahl index (HHI).[5]

HHI is calculated as a sum of square relative shares of companies in the total circulation of the branch:

$$\text{HHI} = s_1^2 + s_2^2 + \ldots + s_n^2 = \sum_{i=1}^{n} s_i^2$$

where s_i represents a relative share of i-company in the total circulation of a branch.

In the upper index, by adding squares of relative shares of the companies in the total sale of the branch, we increase a relative share of the bigger ones, and reduce the relative share of smaller companies in the sum, which shows a relatively higher power of big companies. Therefore, for HHI it stands that:

$$s_i > s_i^2, i = 1,\ldots,n \quad i \quad 0 < s_i < 1, \text{ so:}$$

$$\sum_{i=1}^{n} s_i = 1 \text{ and } \sum_{i=1}^{n} s_i^2 < 1, \text{ i.e.:}$$

$$\sum_{i=1}^{n} s_i > \sum_{i=1}^{n} s_i^2$$

As s_i is higher in the interval $0 < s_i < 1$, i.e. closer to 1, the difference between s_i i s_i^2 is less, and vice versa. This also stands for the relative sums. By using these features of the relationship between the quantities and the relation presented, for the needs of our analysis, we have formulated the *index of relative concentration of power* (IRC) of *i*-subject as:

$$\text{IRC}_i = \frac{s_i^2}{\displaystyle\sum_{i=1}^{n} s_i^2} \tag{1.4}$$

Therefore, IRC measures a relative significance of the square share of *i*-subject in the sum of square shares of all the participants of one community (groups, branches) in a common quantity (e.g. values of branch sale, GDP, etc.). By the character of value relations, IRC_i will be higher than s_i for those subjects whose relative share in the value of the phenomena observed is above average. Vice versa also stands. The sum of all the values of IRC is:

$$\sum_{i=1}^{n} \frac{s_i^2}{\displaystyle\sum_{i=1}^{n} s_i^2} = \sum_{i=1}^{n} \text{IRC}_i = 1 \tag{1.5}$$

Let's remind that $\displaystyle\sum_{i=1}^{n} s_i = 1$, i.e.:

$$\sum_{i=1}^{n} \text{IRC}_i = \sum_{i=1}^{n} s_i = 1 \tag{1.6}$$

Therefore, by using IRC, the same value of a phenomenon was divided among the same subjects proportionally to their relative power that is implied by IRC. Thus, the sum of IRC equals one.

If there is an equality of the distribution of some quantity to all the members of a community, then there is no difference in their relative power:

$$s_1 = s_2 = \ldots = s_n \Rightarrow \text{IRC}_1 = \text{IRC}_2 = \ldots = \text{IRC}_n \tag{1.7}$$

Let us return to our concrete example for the subjects A and B. By using the explained, we will have:

$$s_A^2 + s_B^2 < 1, \text{ where:}$$

$$s_A^2 < s_A \ i \ s_B^2 < s_B, \text{ as well as:}$$

$$\text{IRC}_A = \frac{s_A^2}{s_A^2 + s_B^2} > s_A \quad \text{and} \quad \text{IRC}_B = \frac{s_B^2}{s_A^2 + s_B^2} < s_B$$

Therefore, $\text{IRC}_A > s_A$, while $\text{IRC}_B < s_B$ because $s_A > s_B$ and, simultaneously, $s_A + s_B = 1$ and $\text{IRC}_A + \text{IRC}_B = 1$, where $\text{IRC}_A > \text{IRC}_B$.

For example, if $k_A = 0.7$ and $k_B = 0.3$, i.e. $s_A = 0.7$ (70%) and $s_B = 0.3$ (30%), then $s_A^2 = 0.49$ and $s_B^2 = 0.09$, so $s_A^2 + s_B^2 = 0.49 + 0.09 = 0.58$ < 1. Relative share s_A^2 was increased, and s_B^2 was reduced in the sum $s_A^2 + s_B^2$ in relation to a relative share s_A and s_B in the sum $s_A + s_B$:

$$s_A^* = \frac{s_A^2}{s_A^2 + s_B^2} = \frac{0.49}{0.58} = 0.845 > s_A \quad i \quad s_B^* = \frac{s_B^2}{s_A^2 + s_B^2} = \frac{0.09}{0.58} = 0.155 < s_B$$

This example of calculating a relative power of the subjects A and B can be illustrated as shown in the following graph (Figure 1.1).

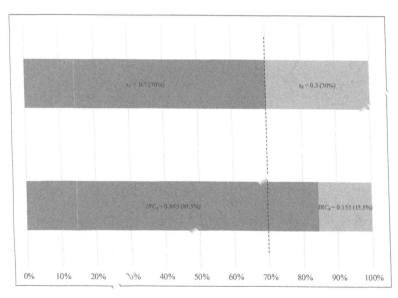

Figure 1.1   Relative structure and IRC.

1.10.3.3 Application of Models

For each subject that is a member of a community (group, branch, union, etc.) we can determine the value of IRC in the distribution of a certain quantity. Based on different features of the subjects, we can perform their grouping according to similarity. By adding the values of IRC for the members of the same group, we will obtain the value of IRC for the group. By comparing the values of IRC of the groups, we will reach the conclusion on distribution of relative power between them regarding the share in distribution of the values of a certain phenomenon.

As it was previous explained, in this analysis we will examine the change in concentration of economic power for 190 countries ($i = 1,..., 190$), from which 105 small ones ($m, j = 1,..., 105$) and 85 big countries ($v, l = 1,..., 85$), so there must the following be valid:

$$\sum_{j=1}^{105} \mathrm{IRC}_j + \sum_{l=1}^{85} \mathrm{IRC}_l = \mathrm{IRC}_m + \mathrm{IRC}_v = 1$$

Analysis of the concentration of economic power in the EU, based on the data of Eurostat on GDP of member countries of the Union for the period from 2000 to 2015, has shown that a relative economic power of small countries grows in the EU (Tomaš & Radović-Marković, 2018). This knowledge will be verified for small countries of the EU, by using the data of IMF on GDP for the period from 1980 to 2017 and compare it with the state for small countries in the world. We will examine changes of the concentration of relative economic power for the members of the EU ($i = 1,..., 28$), which will be classified into "small" (m), where ($j = 1,..., 16$) and "big" (v), where ($l = 1, ..., 12$). According to that, it stands:

$$\sum_{j=1}^{16} \mathrm{IRC}_j + \sum_{l=1}^{12} \mathrm{IRC}_l = \mathrm{IRC}_m + \mathrm{IRC}_v = 1$$

By comparing the values obtained for IRC_m and IRC_v, based on GDP distribution in the period from 1980 to 2017, we will reach the conclusion on the change in concentration of economic power between a great number of small and a lesser number of big countries. By the presented method of the analysis, with the other criteria of grouping the countries, we will follow the changes in power concentration between Eastern Asia and Western hemisphere; more significant economic regions of the world (North America, West Europe,

West hemisphere, the EU, G7); emerging and developing markets (Asia, Europe, developing countries); the three most significant economic regions of the world (Asia and Pacific, North America, the EU); and specific groups of countries within the EU (Eastern Europe, Western Europe, European countries in development, and Eurozone countries). One of the goals of European policy of the convergence of economic systems is the elimination or reduction of bad influence on development that comes from the size of the country. This is the chance to verify whether that goal is achieved.

1.11 The Results of the Analysis

Modern globalization leads to changes in the concentration of economic power by regions, country groups, and hemispheres (Table A.2). The relative economic power of the most developed countries and the most developed regions of the world is gradually weakening (Figure 1.2). In the period from 1980 to 1991 developed countries achieved a high concentration of economic power, above 75%, with the tendency of continuous growth, to reach the maximum IRC value of 83.6% in 1992. The following years led to its gradual decrease, so that the same countries in 2017 reached

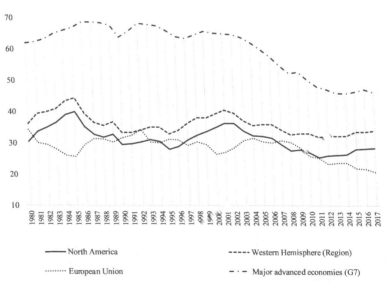

Figure 1.2 IRC – the most developed countries and regions of the world.

60.1% of the total economic power of the world. The greatest influence on the demonstrated movement of relative economic power in the developed countries of the world has the tendency of decreasing the concentration of power in the group of developed G7 countries.

In the period from 1980 to 1986, the IRC for the G7 showed continuous growth, from 61.7% in 1980 to 68.6% in 1986. Until 2005, the IRC held a value above 60%, and fell for the first time in that year under 60% and in the following years continued, with a short-term shift upwards, a continuous decline. In 2010, G7's relative power fell for the first time below 50% and it maintained at that level by the end of 2017 (46.2%). Similar tendencies can also be registered for North America, the Western hemisphere, the EU, and Western Europe, observing them as special economic regions.

The three major world economic regions Asia and the Pacific, North America, and the EU concentrate together about 85% of the world's economic power (Figure 1.3).

Region Asia and the Pacific show the tendency of relative economic power, while the North American and EU countries have been reducing their relative economic power for more than a decade.

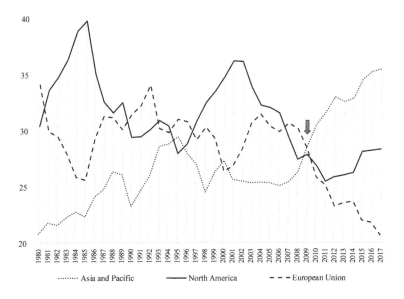

Figure 1.3 IRC – Asia and the Pacific, North America, and the European Union.

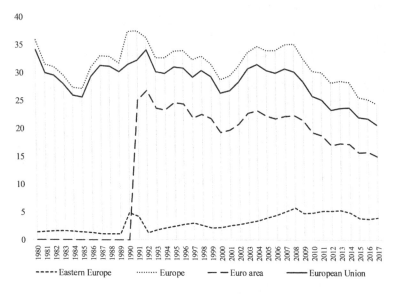

Figure 1.4   IRC – Europe and the European Union.

The relative economic power of these three regions got equalized in 2009. That year the world economy was in a very serious crisis.

In the following years, following the implementation of a series of state intervention measures, which did not always confirm the accustomed consistency, the North American region managed to slow down the decline in relative economic power reduction, while the EU failed. At the same time, Asia and the Pacific continue to strengthen relative economic power. In 1980, the EU recorded a maximum value of IRC (34.1%). Almost the same value was reached only in 1992 (Figure 1.4).

The recovery of its relative power lasted from 2000 to 2004, after which the tendency of weakening occurred. At the end of 2017, the value of its IRC was 20.7%. The same tendencies were also recorded in the countries of the Eurozone. The quantitative easing program of the European Central Bank obviously had no effect on improving the relative economic power of the EU. The dominant character of the EU has affected the values of IRC for the whole of Europe. The countries of Eastern Europe showed a tendency to strengthen relative economic power after 1992. Their small share in the total GDP of Europe could not significantly improve the relative economic power of Europe.

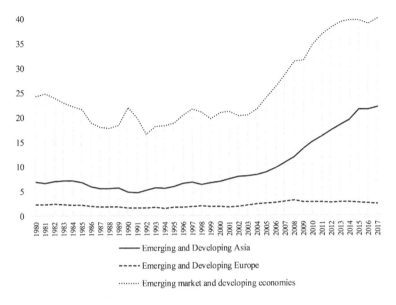

Figure 1.5 IRC – emerging markets and emerging economies.

The weakening of the relative economic power of developed countries and regions is accompanied by the strengthening of the relative economic power of developing countries and emerging markets (Figure 1.5).

The relative economic power of these countries has grown rapidly since the beginning of the 21st century. Their IRC had the lowest value of 16.4% in 1992. In the following years, the value continued to grow with fewer declines in 1999 and 2003, so this group of countries reached the value of IRC in 2017 of 39.9%. The crucial importance for such an IRC value stream has a continuing growth in the relative economic power of Asian developing countries and countries with emerging markets. European developing countries and emerging markets have had an almost neutral impact on the growth of the economic power of this group of countries.

The five most economically powerful countries in the world: The United States, Japan, Germany, France and the United Kingdom, concentrated, on average, 94.6% (IRC 5) of the world's global economic power from 1980 to 2005. At the end of 2005, China entered the five most powerful countries in the world, measured by IRC, and France was out of the group. In the next two years (2006–2007), the relative economic power of China, the United Kingdom, and

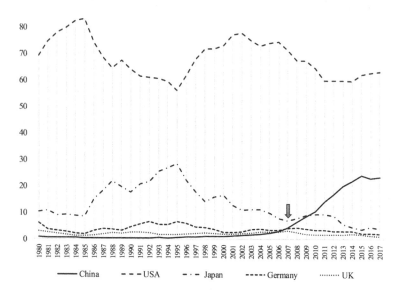

Figure 1.6   IRC – five of the most economically powerful countries.

Germany is almost equalized (Figure 1.6). At the same time, starting from 1995, Japan's relative economic power weakens.

After entering China into the group of the five most powerful countries in the world, the average value of their IRC for the period 2005–2017 drops to 91%. This decrease is the result of a relatively greater decline in economic power, primarily of the United States and Japan, relative to China's relative power growth, but also the consequence of strengthening the economic power of other countries in the world.

Throughout the analyzed period, the United States represented the economically most powerful country of the world. Their IRC had a maximum value in 1985 when it was 83%, and ten years later it recorded a minimum value of 56%. The average value of the analyzed period from 1980 to 2017 was 68.4%. Such an IRC value confirms the dominant role of the United States in launching and determining the basic tendencies of functioning of the entire world economy. Indeed, by such a position, the United States concentrate a large part of the world's wealth, but it is also the fact that no other country in the world would be able to conquer its existing wealth level without the contributions that the United States produced in the process of global wealth.

Since 2010, China has been the second most economically powerful country in the world. The minimum IRC value of 0.28% was recorded in 1991. Until 2000, the concentration of relative economic power for the most populous country of the world was below 1%. In the coming years, IRC grew rapidly and reached a maximum of 24% in 2016. The average value of IRC China for the analyzed period was 5.2%, which confirms the fact that China's current economic power can thank the development over the last 15 years.

The United States and China since 2010 are the two most economically powerful countries in the world (Figure 1.7).

In 2017 these two countries concentrated 86.6% of the total economic power of the world. In addition, the predominant part of the power belongs to the United States. However, in the last 10 years, China recorded higher absolute growth in IRC, which indicates the tendency of reducing the difference in relative economic power between the two most powerful economies of the world (Figure 1.8).

In addition to the above, around the world there have been other changes in the concentration of relative economic power in the world. For example, in 1991, India was the 17th country by value of the IRC, and in 2017 it was 6th. Brazil in 1980 occupied the 80th place by the value of IRC, in 2011 6th, and in 2017 8th place. Russia also

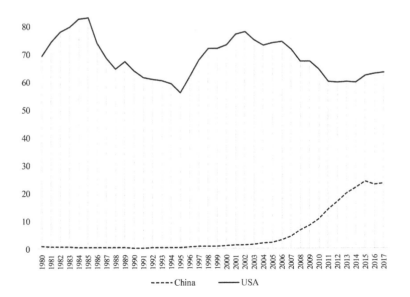

Figure 1.7 IRC – the United States and China.

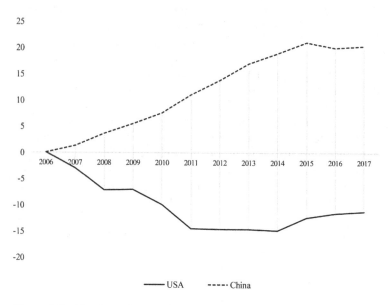

Figure 1.8   Absolute changes in IRC for the United States and China
compared to 2006.

significantly improved its economic power. In 1992, it was the 33rd
economic power of the world, in 2008 it was 8th, and in 2017 11th.

At the end of the analyzed period of change in the concentration
of economic power in the world, in 88 analyzed large countries lived
95.17% of the world population that had 91.75% of the world GDP. At
the same time, in 138 small countries, 4.83% of the world's population lived with 8.25% of the world's GDP. Throughout the analyzed
period (1980–2017) there was no significant change in the relative
GDP structure of the population and the population between large
and small countries. The share of large countries in the distribution of world GDP has always been around 92%. Due to the large
concentration of the population, the average GDP per capita in the
big countries was lower, especially in Congo, Ethiopia, Bangladesh,
Nigeria, India, Indonesia, etc. From the point of view of the concentration of economic power, as we defined in this survey, in large
countries over 99% of the total economic power of the world are
found. In the analyzed period (1980–2017), the lowest concentration
was in 1980 (99.49%), and the highest in 1985 (99.79%). Thus, the
maximum difference of 0.3% of the economic power of the world
arises as a result of the redistribution of income between large and

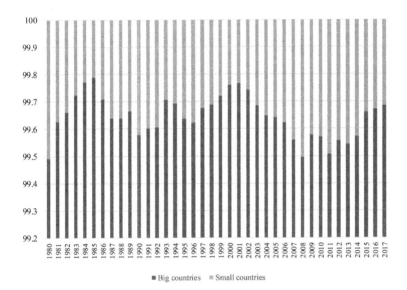

Figure 1.9   IRC for large and small countries in the period from 1980 to 2017.

small countries, alternately, for several years to the benefit of one
and then the other group of countries (Figure 1.9). This can be considered as the usual consequence of market oscillations and market
adjustments. Also, in the group of large countries there are countries whose economic power is smaller than some countries in the
group of small countries, for example: Tanzania, Myanmar, Nepal,
Mozambique, Madagascar, Niger, Burkina Faso, Mali, Malawi,
etc. In the group of small countries there are countries whose IRC
is larger than some countries in the group of large countries, for
example: Sweden, Switzerland, Hong Kong, Austria, United Arab
Emirates, Israel, etc. (Table A.3).

Thus, in general, we cannot confirm that in the conditions of
globalization and the growth of inequality between 1980 and 2017,
there was a strengthening of the economic power of large countries
at the expense of small countries. The analysis of similar tendencies
within the EU has shown that the relative economic power of small
countries grows faster than the relative power of large countries,
as the EU market creates a stronger effect of economies of scale
for small countries (Tomaš & Radović-Marković, 2018). We did not
confirm this tendency for the group of small countries on the world
market: there is no continuous growth or a continuous decline in

the economic power of small or large countries in the global market. Relatively small oscillations of index values are registered, which is a normal consequence of market flexibility. However, economic power is not evenly distributed in both groups of countries, so we can also speak of a change in the concentration of economic power between the countries of both groups.

The relative concentration of economic power within the EU, measured by the same method, in the same period and using the same data sources, shows that the relative economic power of small countries was growing, especially after 1993. Given that the sum of the GDP of 28 members of the EU was viewed as a whole, the growth of the IRC for small countries was followed by a decrease in the value of IRC for large countries (Figures 1.10 and 1.11).

Until 1989 there were no significant changes in the relative economic power between the small and large countries of the EU. The recorded IRC value oscillations can be treated as a consequence of the usual market oscillations. However, from 1989 to 1993, a period of sudden growth of the relative power of large countries occurred. IRC has grown from 98.07% to a maximum of 98.74%.

Figure 1.10   IRC for large countries of the European Union in the period from 1980 to 2017.

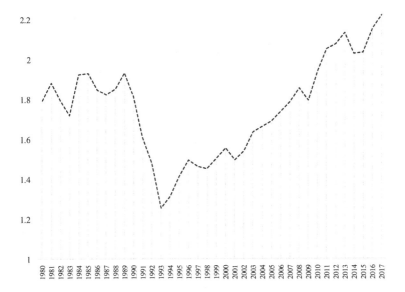

Figure 1.11 IRC for small countries of the European Union in the period from 1980 to 2017.

After that, the growth trend of IRC for small countries ranged from 1.25% in 1993 to 2.22% in 2017. Therefore, the values of the IRC confirm that with the growth of the EU's coherence, the relative economic power of small Union member states is increasing. The business environment of the EU has a positive impact on the growth of the economies of small countries. From the point of view of the growth of the value of the IRC, it can be concluded that this environment gives a stronger impetus to the economic development of the small EU member states than economic globalization gives incentives to small countries that are not members of the EU.

1.12 Conclusion

Globalism is the natural order of things on planet Earth. Due to the limited nature of natural goods and resources that produce economic goods, people have created their communities, set rules for their functioning, set boundaries between them, and set rules of cooperation between them. By this, people have established a global social order that is fundamentally different from the natural global order. The limitation of resources, in terms of human needs, in the natural global order creates conflicts of interest and motivation of people and maintains them in the global social order. Technological and economic development contribute to reducing the rarity of goods needed by people, so people around the world feel that the global world is increasingly a requirement for achieving their motives, which creates the preconditions for homogenizing people's motivation in the world. The degree of globalization is precisely determined by the homogenization of the motivation of people and their communities on the planet Earth. However, globalization does not affect the same and at the same time the homogenization of motivation of individuals, companies, and states. Globalization is a process in which there are a number of opposites, inequalities, and injustices. As long as this is so, we cannot speak of the homogeneity of people's motivation in the world, which is the prerequisite for establishing the equality of the natural and social global order.

Modern globalization is acceptable for companies and investors because it strongly strengthens the role of individuals through innovation and increased productivity. A symbiosis of the interests of individuals, companies, and investors in a global environment can constitute a modern multicultural entrepreneurial environment, which, in relation to the already verified entrepreneurial conditions, is the most liberal and most creative entrepreneurial environment. Potentially, it can offer the unification of all knowledge in the world in the development process with unprecedented opportunities for productivity growth.

Although globalization contributes to reducing production costs, increasing international trade and increasing total wealth, it is not equally acceptable in all parts of the world, in individual markets, and within different social groups. Through economic globalization, competition takes on global dimensions. This establishes new relative price relationships, i.e., labor productivity, which affect the redistribution of wealth between companies, states, regions, social groups, and markets, which affect the change in the concentration of economic power. The present form of globalization does not imply equality between developed and underdeveloped countries, nor between rich and poor people. Regardless of the benefits that globalization brings by the expansion of exchanges, the modern world in which it is pursued is the equity of society, the society of equal opportunities and the society of economic freedom. Globalization helps the world to become economically richest, but with increasing economic and social inequity among people. Economic freedom, competition, regulation, mobility of people, goods, capital, and knowledge contribute to increasing wealth in the global environment, but obviously, the environment modifies them, and ultimately contribute to increasing inequality.

The neoliberal ideology, which forms the basis of the modern phase of globalization, interprets the gap between the rich minority and the poor majority of the population as a fair outcome of competition and market efficiency. It is undeniable that competition has a positive impact on increasing the efficiency of using scarce resources. However, as competition abolishes itself, the degree of competition is changing with the concentration of capital. Market monopolization leads to the transition of competition from the domain of efficiency in the domain of power. The growth of wealth in the world should contribute to increasing economic stability and spreading economic freedom to as much of the humanity as possible. However, this did not happen because many companies, banks, and funds are positioned in the global market so that part of their income is secured by redeployment based on market power. Economists mainly analyze economic stability, economic inequality, and economic freedom at the level of sovereign countries. In the global market, redistribution based on economic power of companies crosses national boundaries, moving economic wealth around the world, while at the same time maintaining and deepening the gap between the rich and the poor. The goal of globalization has never been to establish equality and eliminate poverty in the world. The main goal was determined by large companies to which national markets became too small for development. However, the aspiration of large companies for greater profits and the security of capital placement has led to the expansion of trade, technology transfer, increased labor productivity, poverty reduction, the widening of access to public goods and services, and social development. These are mainly positive external effects of achieving global strategies of multinational companies in new markets. This leads to economic growth in developing countries, but equality is not being established. Due to the unequal conditions of global mobility of goods, labor, capital, and knowledge, in countries with rising markets, the relationships are reproduced, especially in allocation, imposed by investors motivated by maximizing profits. Globalization increases inequality in countries that have been characterized by a lower degree of inequality ("equality in poverty") before the opening of the market. Thus, modern globalization, using, above all, the advantages of opening up the commodity and capital market, on the one hand, and the uneven degree of mobility of production factors on a global scale, on the other hand, leads to the growth of wealth and the widening gap between the rich and the poor in the world. This leads to a change in the concentration of economic power in the world, with an increase in inequality.

The change in the distribution of economic power in the world is seen as an inevitable stage in the globalization of the world economy. Our research has confirmed that there are very significant changes in the distribution of relative economic power in the world for the benefit of developing and emerging markets. This is reflected in the following trends that we have observed on the basis of the movement of the IRC in the analyzed period:

There has been a change in the relative economic power of the entire economic regions, groups of countries and the hemispheres. – Although still dominant in the world, the relative economic power of the most developed countries and the most developed regions of the world is gradually weakening (G7, North America, Western Hemisphere, European Union).

The weakening of the relative economic power of developed countries and regions is accompanied by the strengthening of the relative economic power of developing countries and emerging markets (in particular Asia and the Pacific). In all analyzed economic regions of the world, developing countries and emerging markets have increased their relative power beyond European countries.

According to the IRC values, China has entered the group of the five most economically powerful countries in the world that concentrate more than 90% of the world's economic power, while France has been relatively weakened and lost its place in that group.

Throughout the analyzed period, the United States held the position of the most economically powerful country in the world, influencing decisively the economic flows in the world and even in periods when their economic power was relatively weakened. – Since 2010, China, measured by IRC, has become the second economic power of the world. There is a tendency to reduce the difference in the relative economic power of the two most economically powerful countries.

Although we were expecting it, it was not confirmed that the analyzed phase of globalization has influenced the strengthening of the economic power of small countries, which confirms the limited scope of the economies of the global market economy to small countries. Also, it is obvious that the largest and economically powerful countries in the world have a decisive influence on the functioning of the global economy. However, it is encouraging that the weakening of the economic power of small countries has not been demonstrated.

On the examples of small countries of the European Union it is confirmed that the growth of the coherence of the Union results in the growth of their relative economic power. Thus, the business environment of the European Union develops stronger effects of the economies of scale for small member states than the economic globalization of the world gives impetus to the development of small countries.

Changes in the distribution of economic power around the world cannot be created by themselves. Leading to them in modern conditions are investments. Developing and emerging markets cannot evolve "out of nothing." The release of resources, the opening up of relatively large markets and market reforms in these countries have provided a strong incentive for investment to foreign investors from developed countries. This can in large part be explained by the weakening of the relative economic power of the most developed countries and regions of the world. The registered changes in the distribution of economic power confirm that resource freezing and market opening give an impetus to the spread of economic development in the world and to the increase in total wealth, creating potential preconditions for a better life of people. However, the method of distribution of wealth created is a problem on which there is no agreement. Companies that drive development do so because of their own interests in the conditions of the resource market. Without their motivation for investing, there is no development. They do not deal with the problems of inequality of distribution and social justice. The competition suits them in terms of doing business among states. The fact that among the 100 largest economic entities in the world, measured by total income, is 31 states and 69 companies (Green, 2016) speak much about the situation in the global market. A large number of countries in the world are not in a position to dictate terms of business for large companies. States, especially over the last three decades, prefer to choose economic development and the gap between the rich and the poor than equality in poverty. Time will show whether the change in the distribution of relative economic power, arising therefrom is an inevitable transient state of modern globalization, which should create material assumptions for a richer, freer and fairer world.

The history of socialist countries has confirmed that it is impossible to move from "equality in poverty" to "equality in abundance." This is impossible in the global world. The global world is burdened with contradictions, but, in addition, it creates the largest economic wealth known to human history. This wealth can be the basis for harmonizing the motivation of companies, states and individuals, and the establishment of a global world as a multicultural entrepreneurial environment that has potential opportunities to reduce the contradictions of the global world. Of course, the contradictions of the global world will not be reduced unless the possibilities of redistributing wealth, based on any form of power, are reduced, except for the power of economic efficiency.

Notes

1 The "Kuznets criteria" was applied, that is to say, a small country implies a country of up to 10 million inhabitants. This is discussed in greater detail under point 10 (Method of analysis).
2 This designation is without prejudice to positions on status and is in line with UNSCR 1244 and the ICJ Opinion on the Kosovo* declaration of independence.
3 The Hirschman regional trade concentration index is calculated as the square root of the quadrant export participation in individual countries in the total exports of the observed country.

$$H_i = \sqrt{\sum_s \left(\frac{\sum X_j}{\sum X_n} \right)^2}$$

Where ΣX_j is the export of the analyzed country to the j-th country, ΣX_n is the total export of the observed country or its import to a certain region.
   The value of the index ranges in the interval (0.1). A lower value indicates a higher export dispersion of the analyzed country. The value of the index closer to one signifies the concentration of total exports of a given country to a smaller number of markets.
4 International Economic Association held, in September 1957, an international conference in Hague on the topic "Economic Consequences of the Size of Nations", from which the papers were published in 1960.
5 It is about the index that was in the year 1945 suggested by Hirschman (Hirschman, 1945), and his mathematical form was set in 1950 by Herfindahl (Herfindahl, 1950). Modified form of *HHI* was used for the fisrt time for the calculation of synthetical index of life quality concentration (*SIC*) (Tomaš, 2013a), and *IRC* 2018 for the measurement of a relative concentration of economic power of small countries within European Union (Tomaš & Radović-Marković, 2018).

References

Birdsall, N., 2006. Rising Inequality in the New Global Economy. *International Journal of Development Issues,* 5(1), pp. 1–9.

Carafano, J. J., 2018. Why Small States Matter to Big Powers. [Online] Available at: www.heritage.org/defense/commentary/why-small-states-matter-big-powers [Accessed 7 January 2019].

Chomsky, N., 2002. *On Escalation of Violence in the Middle East* [Interview], 7 May.

Commonwealth Advisory Group, 1997. *A Future for Small States: Overcoming Vulnerability.* London: Commonwealth Secretariat.

Dabla-Norris, E., 2015. *Causes and Consequences of Income Inequality: A Global Perspective.* s.l.: International Monetary Fund.

Dell'Ariccia, G., et al., 2008. *Reaping the Benefits of Financial Globalization.* Washington: International Monetary Fund.

European Commission, 2018. *Strategy for the Western Balkans.* Strasbourg: s.n.

Eurostat, 2018. *Three Quarters of EU Imports from Russia: Energy Products.* Brussels: Eurostat.

Frank, A. G., 1998. *ReORIENT: Global Economy in the Asian Age.* 1st ed. Berkley and Los Angeles: University of California Press.

Frankel, J. A., 2012. What Small Countries Can Teach the World. *Business Economics*, 47(2), pp. 97–103.

Frankel, J. A., & Romer, D., 1999. Does Trade Cause Growth?. *The American Economic Review*, 89(3), pp. 379–399.

Friedman, M., 2002. *Capitalism and Freedom.* Fortieth Anniversary ed. Chicago and London: The University of Chicago Press.

Friedman, T. L., 2005. It's a Flat World, After All. *New York Times Magazine*, 3 April.

Graham, T. E., Levitsky, J. E., Munter, C. P., & Wisner, F. G., 2018. *Time for Action in the Western Balkans: Policy Prescriptions for American Diplomacy.* New York: East West Institute.

Green, D., 2016. From Poverty to Power, The World's Top 100 Economies: 31 Countries; 69 Corporations. [Online] Available at: https://oxfamblogs.org/fp2p/the-worlds-top-100-economies-31-countries-69-corporations/ [Accessed 15 August 2018].

Heath, R., & Gray, A., 2018. Beware Chinese Trojan Horses in the Balkans EU warns. *Politico EU*, 27 July.

Herfindahl, O. C., 1950. *Concentration in the Steel Industry*, Unpublished PhD Dissertation. New York City: Columbia University Press.

Hirschman, A. O., 1945. *National Power and Structure of Foreign Trade.* Berkeley and Los Angeles: University of California Press.

Huntington, S. P., 1991. Democracy's Third Wave. *Journal of Democracy,* 2(2), pp. 12–34.

International Monetary Fund, 2013. *Macroeconomic Issues in Small States and Implications for Fund Engagement.* Washington: IMF.

International Monetary Fund, 2017a. *Staff Guidance Note on the Fund's Engagement with Small Developing States.* Washington: IMF, 24 July 2018.

International Monetary Fund, 2017b. *World Economic Outlook Database.* Washington: IMF.

Kuznets, S., 1957. *Economic Growth of Small Nations.* 1960 ed. New York City: St. Martin's Press.

Laurent, E., 2008. Economic Consequences of the Size of Nations, 50 Years On. [Online] Available at: https://hal-sciencespo.archives-ouvertes.fr/hal-00972823 [Accessed 24 July 2018].

LSE, 2015. *Russia in the Balkans: Research on South Eastern Europe.* London: European Institute, London School of Economics.

LSE Enterprise, 2011. *Study on the Impact of the Single Market on Cohesion: Implications for Cohesion Policy, Growth and Competitiveness, Final Study.* London: London School of Economics.

McMichael, P., 2000. *Development and Social Change: A Global Perspective.* Thousand Oaks, CA: Pine Forge Press.

Mikic, M., & Gilbert, J., 2007. *Trade Statistics in Policymaking: A Handbook of Commonly Used Trade Indices and Indicators.* s.l.: s.n.

Milanovic, B., 2016. *Global Inequality: A New Approach for the Age of Globalization.* London: The Belknap Press of Harvard University Press.

Mises, L. v., 1929. *A Critique of Intervencionism.* Alabama: Ludwig von Mises Institute.

Mogherini, F., 2017. *Remarks by High Representative/Vice-President Federica Mogherini Following the Foreign Affairs Council.* Brussels: Foreign Affairs Council.

Monbiot, G., 2016. The Zombie Doctrine. *The Guardian*, 16 April.

Moore, M., 1995. Democracy and Development in Cross-National Perspective: A New Look at the Statistics. *Democratization,* 2(2), pp. 1–19.

Obama, B., 2016. *President Obama's Final United Nations Speech: Transcript.* New York City: TIME.

Obstfeld, M., 1998. The Global Capital Market: Benefactor or Menace?. *Journal of Economic Perspectives,* 12(4), pp. 9–30.

OECD, 2003. *The Policy Agenda for Growth: An Overview of the Sources of Economic Growth in OECD Countries.* Paris: OECD.

OECD, 2011. *Divided We Stand. Why Inequality Keeps Rising?* Paris: OECD Publishing.

Ostry, J., Loungani, P., & Furceri, D., 2016. *Neoliberalism: Oversold? Finance & Development*, 53(2), pp. 38–41.

Piketty, T., 2014. *Capital in the Twenty-First Century.* 1st ed. Cambridge, MA: The Belknap Press of Harvard University Press.

Pilling, G., 2014. *The Crisis of Keynesian Economics.* Revivals ed. s.l.:Routledge.

Rodrik, D., 2011. *The Globalization Paradox.* New York and London: W.W. Norton.

Sen, A., 1999. *Development as Freedom*. New York: Anchor Books.

Skilling, D., 2012. In Uncertain Seas: Positioning Small Countries to Succeed in a Changing World. [Online] Available at: www.landfall strategy.com/wp-content/uploads/2012/03/Small-countries.pdf [Accessed 8 January 2019].

Stiglitz, J., 2012. *The Price of Inequality: How Today's Divided Society Endangers Our Future*. New York: W. W. Norton & Co.

Stiglitz, J., 2015. Inequality Is holding Back the American Economy. *La Tribune*, 4 September.

Suedosteuropa-Gesellschaft; SWP, 2014. *The Western Balkans – Interests and Policies of the EU, Russia and Turkey*. Berlin: Suedosteuropa-Gesellschaft Muenchen and SWP.

The Economist, 2018. The Western Balkans: Trading Below Potential. *The Economist*, 21 June.

Tomaš, R., 2013a. *"Sintetičko mjerenje kvaliteta života" (Synthetic Measurement of Quality of Life)*. Belgrade: School of Economics, University of Belgrade, pp. 833–838.

Tomaš, R., 2013b. Causes of the Slowed Down and Inefficient Transition of the Economy of Bosnia and Herzegovina and Possibilities of Its Improvement. *Business Excellence,* 7(1), pp. 99–118.

Tomaš, R., & Radović-Marković, M., 2018. Development of Small Countries in the Business Environment of the European Union. *Transylvanian Review of Administrative Sciences*, 53, pp. 84–106.

Vanhanen, T., 1997. *Prospects of Democracy: A Study of 172 Countries*. London and New York: Routledge.

Veenendaal, W. P. & Corbett, J., 2015. Why Small States Offer Important Answers to Large Questions. *Comparative Political Studies,* 48(4), pp. 527–549.

Vieira, S., 2012. *Inequality on the Rise?*. [Online] Available at: www.un.org/en/development/desa/policy/wess/wess_bg_papers/bp_wess2013_svieira1.pdf [Accessed 24 July 2018].

World Bank, 2018. *Poverty and Shared Prosperity 2018: Piecing Together the Poverty Puzzle*. Washington: The World Bank.

World Bank; Independent Evaluation Group (IEG), 2016. *World Bank Group Engagement in Small States: The Cases of the OECS, Pacific Island Countries, Cabo Verde, Djibouti, Mauritius, and the Seychelles—Clustered Country Program Evaluation (CCPE)*. Washington: The World Bank.

Worldometers, 2017. *Elaboration of Data by United Nations, Department of Economic and Social Affairs, Population Division. World Population Prospects: The 2015 Revision. (Medium-fertility variant)*. s.l.: World Population Prospects.

Appendix

Table A.1 Structure of turnover of goods of the Western Balkans in 2017

Country	Albania		Bosnia and Herzegovina		FYR Macedonia		Montenegro		Serbia		Kosovo*		Western Balkans**	
	Export, %	Import, %	Export, %	Import, %	Export, %	Import, %	Export, %	Import, %	Export, %	Import, %	Export, %	Import, %	Export, %	Import, %
EU	77.1	61.6	71.2	61.1	81.1	62.9	35.0	47.0	64.2	60.2	24.9	43.1	58.9	56.0
Western Balkans	14.8	7.9	16.2	12.8	11.7	9.6	41.0	32.0	19.8	4.3	48.4	28.1	25.3	15.8
China	3.1	7.9	0.3	6.5	1.1	5.8	2.0	10.0	0.4	8.0	1.5	9.0	1.4	7.9
Turkey	0.8	8.1	3.9	4.2	1.6	4.8	6.0	3.0	1.8	3.7	1.9	9.6	2.7	5.6
Russia	0.03	1.9	1.3	4.7	1.0	2.0	1.0	0.0	5.7	7.3	0.0	0.8	1.5	2.8
Others	42	12.6	7.1	10.7	3.5	14.9	15.0	8.0	8.1	16.5	23.3	9.4	10.2	12.0
Total	100	100	100	100	100	100	100	100	100	100	100	100	100	100

Source: Calculated by the author based on the data from: https://statistics.cefta.int/goods.
This designation is without prejudice to positions on status, and is in line with UNSCR 1244 and the ICJ Opinion on the Kosovo declaration of independence.
**Average value.

Table A.2 IRC – by region for specified periods

IRC – regions, the average for specified periods

Region	1980–1985	Rank	1986–1990	Rank	1991–1995	Rank	1996–2000	Rank	2001–2005	Rank	2006–2010	Rank	2011–2015	Rank	2016–2017	Rank
Africa (Region)	2.8966824	18	2.6344509	18	2.1514791	19	2.2022683	20	2.0203239	21	2.6863116	22	3.0898982	23	2.8765475	23
Asia and Pacific	21.928022	9	24.893368	8	27.501181	8	26.612505	8	25.434968	8	27.159363	9	32.916835	4	35.33063	4
Australia and New Zealand	1.7663752	25	1.5825315	23	1.4391316	27	1.4554207	26	1.5589626	26	1.8894494	26	2.1656359	27	1.955819	27
Caribbean	0.2311848	30	0.1361598	30	0.126627	32	0.1600813	32	0.1677406	32	0.1746897	32	0.1714642	32	0.1799811	32
Central America	0.2352545	29	0.1588659	29	0.1636344	31	0.1987794	31	0.2137119	31	0.2219507	31	0.2713236	31	0.3258216	31
Central Asia and the Caucasus	0.7829855	28	0.7364059	28	0.8856009	28	0.9698468	29	1.0144825	29	1.5410809	29	1.7493509	29	1.5330922	29
East Asia	14.703477	10	18.807493	10	21.489708	10	20.282962	11	18.811431	11	18.443179	11	22.499621	10	24.449727	8
Eastern Europe	1.4473617	26	1.848436	20	2.3632659	17	2.5531268	18	3.1793541	15	4.9660357	15	4.8782922	16	3.8720635	18
Europe	30.361333	5	33.147761	4	34.561334	3	31.897245	3	32.583358	5	33.402252	4	28.119604	6	24.792243	7
Middle East (Region)	3.5843481	17	3.1330574	17	1.819936	21	2.2278415	19	2.2921324	19	2.9952803	20	3.4136684	20	3.1914681	21
North Africa	1.2296477	27	1.1100193	27	0.6793673	30	0.726389	30	0.6933301	30	0.8431833	30	0.915128	30	0.840094	30
North America	35.647723	4	32.219926	5	29.7541	7	32.092942	4	34.091897	4	28.624176	7	26.32807	7	28.283126	6
Pacific Islands	0.048034	31	0.0349276	31	0.0360574	31	0.0291335	33	0.0233105	33	0.0274347	33	0.0372733	33	0.0375259	33
South America	4.4799041	16	3.6764103	16	3.9215673	15	4.6059725	15	3.1640056	16	4.6919306	16	5.6174952	15	4.9514683	15
South Asia	2.4102767	19	2.064616	19	1.6181577	23	1.8441413	22	2.0648922	20	2.6818665	23	3.2202701	22	3.9130197	17
Southeast Asia	2.2168696	23	1.6673922	22	2.0325235	20	2.0310012	21	1.9618903	23	2.5763528	24	3.244683	21	3.414455	20
Sub-Saharan Africa	2.3025823	20	1.5244326	24	1.4721118	25	1.4758793	25	1.3269934	27	1.8431285	27	2.1747699	26	2.0364808	26
Western Europe (Region)	28.913972	6	31.299326	6	32.198067	5	29.344119	6	29.404004	7	28.436217	8	23.241311	9	20.920178	11
Western Hemisphere (Region)	40.594069	3	36.191362	3	33.965927	4	37.057776	3	37.67355	3	33.712747	3	32.388352	5	33.740397	5
ASEAN-5	2.0602554	24	1.4995977	25	1.7649307	22	1.6939779	24	1.6345881	25	2.154912	25	2.7091522	24	2.9028168	22
Advanced economies	76.787301	1	81.093621	1	81.839723	1	79.402953	1	78.669262	1	69.760786	1	61.442106	1	60.676206	1

(Continued)

IRC – regions, the average for specified periods

Region	1980–1985	Rank	1986–1990	Rank	1991–1995	Rank	1996–2000	Rank	2001–2005	Rank	2006–2010	Rank	2011–2015	Rank	2016–2017	Rank
Commonwealth of Independent States	0	32	0	32	0.8628669	29	1.3468122	28	1.6736376	24	3.1057385	19	3.455227	19	2.4804592	24
Emerging and Developing Asia	6.8571314	12	5.4290988	12	5.3056338	14	6.5641122	14	7.9369819	13	12.008367	12	18.404676	11	21.651653	9
Emerging and Developing Europe	2.2303486	22	1.7394423	21	1.5308934	24	1.7748418	23	2.0105206	22	2.7001297	21	2.559913	25	2.3577258	25
Emerging market and developing economies	23.2127	8	18.906381	9	18.160277	11	20.597047	10	21.330739	10	30.239215	5	38.557894	3	39.323794	3
Euro area	0	32	0	32	24.641481	9	21.934851	9	21.67228	9	21.376135	10	17.18188	12	15.409371	12
European Union	28.811631	7	30.647701	7	31.468446	6	29.190956	7	29.515229	6	28.98245	6	23.51761	8	21.245641	10
Latin America and the Caribbean	6.9159918	11	5.1074799	13	5.8247424	13	6.5929439	13	5.4861907	14	6.785838	14	7.6707028	14	6.7850137	14
Major advanced economies (G7)	64.101179	2	67.307933	2	66.933856	2	64.550107	2	63.056208	2	53.477469	2	46.632054	2	46.62854	2
Middle East and North Africa	4.6452505	15	4.0619398	15	2.2298999	18	2.6296711	17	2.7033711	18	3.6014933	18	4.053242	18	3.7480906	19
Middle East, North Africa, Afghanistan, and Pakistan	4.9700846	14	4.317418	14	2.4816943	16	2.8823942	16	2.9484936	17	3.8880083	17	4.3938816	17	4.1584391	16
Other advanced economies	6.8137372	13	7.3986736	11	8.0859634	12	8.3384984	12	8.4626112	12	8.7139303	13	8.9288602	13	8.7035851	13
Sub-Saharan Africa	2.239145	21	1.4652171	26	1.446464	26	1.4359417	27	1.2749136	28	1.7511333	28	2.0734926	28	1.8905019	28

Table A.3 The IRC movement in the period of 1980–2015, the average value and its ranking for the indicated periods

Country (ranking according to the number of inhabitants 2017)	IRC, average for periods												
	1980–1985	Rank	1986–1990	Rank	1991–1995	Rank	1996–2000	Rank	2000–2005	Rank	2006–2010	Rank	2011–2015	Rank
I Large countries													
1 China	0.5790587	8	0.353173	8	0.3997308	9	0.8867742	7	1.6783542	6	6.600521	3	19.350778	2
2 India	0.2748833	10	0.20938	13	0.1197592	16	0.159776	13	0.2224078	13	0.5562778	12	0.796018	10
3 United States	77.753808	1	67.64057	1	59.628476	1	69.263596	1	75.317306	1	68.9819	1	60.24366	1
4 Indonesia	0.0724018	20	0.030967	25	0.0466088	24	0.0378214	25	0.0332822	23	0.1010648	18	0.174023	16
5 Brazil	0.1921888	13	0.325927	11	0.339869	10	0.5236676	8	0.2235434	12	0.868118	8	1.2422242	7
6 Pakistan	0.0088048	40	0.005607	41	0.0056936	40	0.0056016	45	0.0048136	45	0.0084878	49	0.0120298	46
7 Nigeria		–	0.001384	59	0.0075322	38	0.0208634	31	0.0071962	40	0.0288818	32	0.0517026	26
8 Bangladesh	0.0031642	54	0.002328	51	0.0019668	52	0.00223	52	0.0021772	54	0.0031552	58	0.0058562	57
9 Russia		–	0.352472	9	0.2930952	11	0.100353	16	0.1539014	16	0.684576	11	0.8740018	9
10 Mexico	0.3475557	9	0.11201	16	0.2392732	12	0.232086	11	0.3223948	10	0.3374978	14	0.3181754	15
11 Japan	9.3649165	2	18.47879	2	24.584404	2	17.281922	2	11.148929	2	8.2002438	2	6.4510908	3
12 Ethiopia	0.0004277	70	0.000317	66	0.0001735	75	5.96E-05	95	4.88E-05	104	0.0002091	91	0.0005146	82
13 Philippines	0.0089205	39	0.004189	43	0.0051316	41	0.0059842	44	0.0041692	48	0.0086824	48	0.0150006	41
14 Viet Nam	0.0046047	48	0.002109	52	0.0002328	70	0.0006374	60	0.0010044	59	0.002752	61	0.0060126	56
15 Egypt	0.0072697	42	0.01841	31	0.003363	47	0.0064064	43	0.0047284	46	0.0096738	46	0.0180648	37
16 DR Congo	0.0203283	30	0.003577	45	0.0017396	53	0.0005302	61	5.07E-05	102	0.0001033	104	0.000218	95
17 Iran	0.113442	17	0.298509	12	0.0336782	25	0.0464604	25	0.0264742	27	0.0449748	27	0.0411692	28
18 Germany	3.3372643	3	3.725326	3	5.8812498	3	4.2378558	3	3.2734506	3	3.826418	4	2.912366	4
19 Turkey	0.053033	18	0.047361	21	0.060911	22	0.0580154	21	0.0613528	18	0.1521292	17	0.1708008	17
20 Thailand	0.0092545	38	0.010006	34	0.0216022	29	0.0173632	32	0.0129124	36	0.0256372	33	0.0342754	30
21 United Kingdom	1.9742977	5	2.046762	5	1.9490656	5	2.0486448	5	2.3189732	4	2.4259848	5	1.6485736	5

(Continued)

IRC, average for periods

Country (ranking according to the number of inhabitants 2017)	1980–1985	Rank	1986–1990	Rank	1991–1995	Rank	1996–2000	Rank	2000–2005	Rank	2006–2010	Rank	2011–2015	Rank
22 France	2.355595	4	2.456761	4	2.482791	4	1.8882282	5	1.8000382	5	2.3176346	6	1.619546	6
23 Italy	1.3013935	6	1.926878	6	1.7991612	6	1.3058736	6	1.2840526	7	1.5549488	7	0.9607284	8
24 Tanzania	0.0005302	66	0.000123	77	1.85E-05	110	7.06E-05	93	0.0001158	86	0.0002134	90	0.000382	90
25 South Africa	0.0408532	24	0.020874	30	0.023674	27	0.0171098	34	0.0180238	31	0.0307726	31	0.0303066	32
26 Myanmar	—	—	—	—	—	—	3.89E-05	104	6.27E-05	99	0.000367	83	0.0008026	72
27 South Korea	0.0421207	23	0.092679	19	0.2124454	13	0.228435	12	0.2652998	11	0.3493512	13	0.3651352	14
28 Colombia	0.0167752	34	0.00702	40	0.008521	36	0.0110562	38	0.0067476	42	0.0169786	39	0.0269452	33
29 Kenya	0.0005425	64	0.000327	65	0.000142	78	0.0001714	78	0.0001586	83	0.0003824	82	0.000637	79
30 Spain	0.2484393	11	0.340733	10	0.4242916	8	0.3174538	10	0.4385804	9	0.7060856	9	0.401148	13
31 Ukraine	—	—	—	—	0.0010542	57	0.0015272	55	0.0018914	56	0.0067012	51	0.0051306	59
32 Argentina	0.1555227	15	0.037909	24	0.0802006	19	0.0808554	17	0.021359	29	0.0357028	28	0.0730522	21
33 Sudan	0.00037	72	0.000338	64	3.35E-05	102	0.0001014	88	0.0001924	80	0.000856	69	0.001039	68
34 Uganda	0.0003028	75	0.000128	76	1.94E-05	107	3.19E-05	107	3.01E-05	113	8.61E-05	107	0.0001358	104
35 Algeria	0.0144515	36	0.008751	35	0.0027924	49	0.002025	53	0.0029694	52	0.0068326	50	0.0087016	51
36 Iraq	—	—	—	—	—	—	0.0001639	79	0.0004698	65	0.003855	57	0.0096644	48
37 Poland	0.0270693	27	0.011616	33	0.0124942	35	0.0226794	28	0.029623	26	0.0647244	23	0.0575986	23
38 Canada	0.6522503	7	0.588324	7	0.448963	7	0.368307	9	0.4576178	8	0.7011272	10	0.6762268	11
39 Morocco	0.0020603	57	0.001495	58	0.001488	55	0.0014106	56	0.0014286	58	0.0023818	62	0.0023058	62
40 Afghanistan	—	—	—	—	—	—	—	—	0.0000106	132	3.82E-05	120	8.34E-05	110
41 Saudi Arabia	0.1428302	16	0.021912	29	0.0234206	28	0.0224902	29	0.0303104	24	0.0674464	22	0.1099422	19
42 Peru	0.0028525	55	0.002941	49	0.001975	51	0.0023966	50	0.0020564	55	0.0044388	56	0.007773	52
43 Venezuela	0.0334728	25	0.007252	39	0.0047736	43	0.0071172	41	0.0070304	41	0.0196444	37	0.0172284	39
44 Malaysia	0.0058167	45	0.003434	46	0.0065232	39	0.0078852	39	0.0080864	39	0.0150242	40	0.0212912	35
45 Uzbekistan	—	—	—	—	4.06E-05	96	0.0001856	76	0.0000737	98	0.0002672	87	0.0006838	76

#	Country														
46	Mozambique	0.0001322	82	4.33E−05	94	8.56E−06	122	1.63E−05	117	1.89E−05	118	3.42E−05	122	4.97E−05	118
47	Nepal	3.68E−05	99	3.04E−05	98	2.30E−05	104	0.0000234	112	2.48E−05	117	4.88E−05	115	8.33E−05	111
48	Ghana	0.0076722	41	0.000193	72	0.0001381	80	0.0001063	86	8.70E−05	91	0.0002266	89	0.0003686	91
49	Yemen		−	5.72E−05	87	0.0004874	61	0.0000454	101	8.65E−05	92	0.000201	93	0.0003088	92
50	Angola	0.0002295	76	0.000198	71	7.79E−05	83	4.35E−05	102	0.0001601	82	0.0015852	64	0.0028574	61
51	Madagascar	7.86E−05	91	2.01E−05	104	1.16E−05	118	1.19E−05	121	1.27E−05	129	2.07E−05	134	2.23E−05	136
52	Australia	0.2082887	12	0.16139	14	0.1425178	15	0.1408176	15	0.1641128	15	0.3325396	15	0.4626424	12
53	Cameroon	0.0004542	67	0.000436	62	0.0001926	72	7.91E−05	91	9.70E−05	90	0.0001556	99	0.0001764	100
54	Côte d'Ivoire	0.0004108	71	0.000249	68	0.0001412	79	0.0001204	83	0.0001153	87	0.0001638	97	0.0001982	97
55	Taiwan	0.0172978	33	0.037915	23	0.069146	21	0.0761026	18	0.0600156	19	0.0552814	24	0.0558668	25
56	Niger	2.58E−05	103	1.21E−05	113	5.70E−06	126	2.85E−06	139	3.59E−06	142	7.90E−06	143	1.14E−05	144
57	Sri Lanka	0.0002222	77	0.000169	75	0.0001896	73	0.0002708	71	0.0002712	74	0.0006448	76	0.0011686	67
58	Romania	0.0157628	35	0.00747	38	0.0010282	58	0.0011928	57	0.0023268	53	0.009376	47	0.0074216	53
59	Burkina Faso	1.98E−05	106	1.57E−05	107	1.09E−05	119	6.08E−06	134	9.29E−06	133	1.95E−05	135	2.83E−05	131
60	Syria	0.001909	58	0.001286	60	0.000254	67	0.000253	72	0.0003136	71	0.0007684	73	−	−
61	Mali	1.68E−05	108	1.54E−05	108	1.32E−05	114	9.05E−06	130	1.24E−05	130	2.75E−05	126	3.78E−05	124
62	Chile	0.0043072	50	0.001587	57	0.0034596	46	0.0053292	47	0.00422	47	0.0105804	45	0.0146852	43
63	Malawi	0.0000279	102	1.39E−05	110	1.29E−05	115	1.12E−05	124	6.27E−06	139	9.59E−06	140	9.10E−06	146
64	Kazakhstan		−		−	9.19E−05	82	0.000343	69	0.0007148	60	0.004487	55	0.0094634	49
65	Zambia	9.62E−05	86	2.79E−05	99	1.71E−05	111	1.16E−05	122	0.000017	123	8.48E−05	108	0.0001372	103
66	Netherlands	0.161898	14	0.15472	15	0.170369	14	0.1550558	14	0.1711024	14	0.232618	16	0.1557198	18
67	Guatemala	0.0004432	68	0.000116	78	0.0001438	77	0.0002214	73	0.0002774	73	0.000436	81	0.000645	78
68	Ecuador	0.0018073	60	0.000415	63	0.0004036	62	0.0004798	62	0.0005842	64	0.001116	67	0.001851	65
69	Zimbabwe	0	147	2.76E−05	100	6.58E−05	90	7.85E−05	92	4.33E−05	106	1.89E−05	136	3.65E−05	125
70	Cambodia	0	147	4.17E−07	132	8.46E−06	124	9.94E−06	128	1.32E−05	127	3.01E−05	123	0.0000504	117
71	Senegal	0.000061	95	6.05E−05	84	3.65E−05	99	0.0000204	115	2.51E−05	116	0.000047	116	4.55E−05	120
72	Chad	4.62E−06	121	5.48E−06	121	3.67E−06	133	2.67E−06	140	8.54E−06	135	2.84E−05	125	0.000034	127
73	Guinea	1.83E−05	107	1.27E−05	111	1.39E−05	113	1.08E−05	126	5.61E−06	140	5.79E−06	148	7.54E−06	147
74	South Sudan													4.50E−05	121
75	Rwanda	1.46E−05	110	1.42E−05	109	3.69E−06	132	2.49E−06	142	2.12E−06	148	7.03E−06	144	0.0000122	142

(Continued)

IRC, average for periods

Country (ranking according to the number of inhabitants 2017)	1980–1985	Rank	1986–1990	Rank	1991–1995	Rank	1996–2000	Rank	2000–2005	Rank	2006–2010	Rank	2011–2015	Rank
76 Burundi	6.80E–06	120	3.40E–06	126	1.38E–06	143	6.73E–07	155	4.51E–07	164	8.54E–07	162	1.47E–06	161
77 Tunisia	0.0005395	65	0.000308	67	0.0003504	63	0.0003916	67	0.0004048	70	0.0005546	77	0.0004498	86
78 Benin	9.90E–06	112	6.85E–06	117	5.49E–06	128	5.07E–06	136	7.91E–06	136	1.38E–05	137	1.60E–05	138
79 Belgium	0.0621118	21	0.059255	20	0.0700028	20	0.0569952	22	0.0543428	21	0.073918	20	0.0559334	24
80 Bolivia	0.0000862	89	4.96E–05	93	4.32E–05	95	0.0000545	98	3.99E–05	107	8.21E–05	110	0.00019	98
82 Greece	0.0173907	32	0.013535	32	0.0171034	32	0.0172392	33	0.0211726	30	0.03288	30	0.0130242	45
83 Dominican Republic	0.0007108	62	0.000188	73	0.0002406	69	0.0004142	65	0.0004238	68	0.0007092	75	0.0008474	71
84 Czech Republic	–	–	–	–	0.0006762	59	0.0034672	59	0.0055624	48	0.0129492	42	0.0094496	50
85 Portugal	0.0057677	46	0.007505	37	0.0131234	34	0.0124848	36	0.0142966	35	0.018774	38	0.0109328	47
II Small countries														
86 Azerbaijan	–	–	–	–	3.09E–06	136	1.50E–05	119	0.0000376	110	0.0005306	79	0.0009792	70
87 Sweden	0.0895812	18	0.095489	18	0.0814496	18	0.0614326	20	0.056418	20	0.0719914	21	0.0660724	22
88 Hungary	0.0032625	53	0.002063	53	0.002041	50	0.0019054	54	0.0039354	49	0.00595	52	0.003828	60
89 Belarus	–	–	–	–	0.0001518	76	0.0001618	80	0.0002316	76	0.0008672	68	0.0009954	69
90 United Arab Emirates	0.0104733	37	0.003204	48	0.0038116	45	0.005496	46	0.009692	37	0.0234194	34	0.0305206	31
91 Tajikistan	–	–	–	–	3.56E–07	155	1.06E–06	152	1.49E–06	152	6.63E–06	146	1.36E–05	141
92 Serbia	–	–	–	–	–	–	0.0001751	77	0.0002232	77	0.0005406	78	0.000402	89
93 Austria	0.0329663	26	0.040813	22	0.0500806	23	0.039711	23	0.0362172	24	0.0494416	26	0.0376996	29
94 Switzerland	0.0786893	19	0.099404	17	0.101775	17	0.0737504	17	0.0656616	19	0.087165	19	0.101177	20

No.	Country													
95	Israel	0.0045273	49	0.004945	42	0.0078386	37	0.0115564	37	0.0095572	38	0.012839	43	0.0173142	38
96	Honduras	0.0001068	84	8.36E-05	80	2.82E-05	103	3.15E-05	108	3.86E-05	109	5.90E-05	112	0.0000774	112
97	Papua New Guinea	9.54E-05	87	5.25E-05	90	6.22E-05	92	3.48E-05	106	1.76E-05	121	4.00E-05	119	9.19E-05	108
98	Jordan	0.0001337	81	8.75E-05	79	3.91E-05	97	4.96E-05	99	0.0000609	100	0.0001445	100	0.0002386	94
99	Togo	4.22E-06	122	4.84E-06	123	3.16E-06	135	1.94E-06	146	1.59E-06	150	2.68E-06	155	3.71E-06	156
100	Hong Kong	0.0063138	44	0.008439	36	0.01744	31	0.023812	27	0.016047	32	0.0149188	41	0.0164986	40
101	Bulgaria	0.0047977	47	0.00269	50	6.62E-05	89	0.0001178	84	0.000252	75	0.0007302	74	0.0006538	77
102	Laos	8.14E-05	116	2.54E-06	127	2.56E-06	139	2.29E-06	143	2.34E-06	146	8.65E-06	141	2.39E-05	135
103	Paraguay	0.0001615	79	5.81E-05	86	7.32E-05	85	0.0000705	94	3.09E-05	111	0.0000826	109	0.0001612	101
104	Sierra Leone	2.20E-05	104	5.19E-06	122	1.72E-06	142	1.08E-06	151	1.01E-06	155	1.76E-06	157	3.91E-06	154
105	Libya	0.0072122	43	0.001618	56	0.0013392	56	0.0010414	58	0.000589	63	0.0014962	65	0.0006888	75
106	Nicaragua	5.01E-05	96	3.33E-05	97	1.88E-05	108	1.80E-05	116	1.73E-05	122	2.08E-05	133	2.64E-05	132
107	El Salvador	6.82E-05	93	2.30E-05	102	6.33E-05	91	0.0001154	85	0.0001274	85	0.0001368	103	0.0001282	105
108	Kyrgyzstan	0	147	0	155	1.05E-06	145	2.15E-06	145	2.06E-06	149	0.000006	147	1.01E-05	145
109	Lebanon	8.84E-05	88	2.30E-05	103	0.0000717	86	0.000217	74	0.000215	78	0.0002928	84	0.0004628	85
110	Singapore	0.0016453	61	0.001801	54	0.0050636	42	0.0072794	40	0.0059066	43	0.0118122	44	0.0186464	36
111	Denmark	0.0254677	28	0.030765	26	0.030107	26	0.0261918	26	0.0253622	28	0.0335664	29	0.0242186	34
112	Finland	0.017962	31	0.027384	27	0.0168204	33	0.014381	35	0.015515	33	0.0208136	35	0.0148898	42
113	Turkmenistan	–	–	–	–	1.88E-05	109	9.56E-06	129	0.000076	95	0.000166	96	0.0002894	93
114	Eritrea	–	–	–	–	3.78E-07	152	4.93E-07	156	4.54E-07	163	8.32E-07	163	2.78E-06	157
115	Slovakia	–	–	–	–	0.0001792	74	0.0003918	66	0.0006608	61	0.0022234	63	0.00199	64
116	Norway	0.0254487	29	0.0239	28	0.0213636	30	0.0220468	30	0.0299006	25	0.053698	25	0.0514816	27
117	Central African Republic	3.41E-06	123	4.42E-06	124	2.20E-06	141	8.25E-07	153	6.76E-07	158	1.09E-06	161	7.67E-07	162
118	State of Palestine	–	–	–	–	–	–	–	–	–	–	–	–	–	–
119	Costa Rica	8.16E-05	90	5.87E-05	85	0.0001111	81	0.0001488	81	0.0001712	81	0.0002912	85	0.0005218	81

(Continued)

Country (ranking according to the number of inhabitants 2017)

IRC, average for periods

Country (ranking according to the number of inhabitants 2017)	1980–1985	Rank	1986–1990	Rank	1991–1995	Rank	1996–2000	Rank	2000–2005	Rank	2006–2010	Rank	2011–2015	Rank
120 Congo	1.65 E−05	109	1.23 E−05	112	8.23 E−06	125	5.15 E−06	135	8.93 E−06	134	2.93 E−05	124	3.86 E−05	123
121 Ireland	0.0027395	56	0.003281	47	0.003877	44	0.0066264	42	0.0142996	34	0.020264	36	0.0133124	44
122 Oman	0.0004295	69	0.000209	70	0.000199	71	0.0002138	75	0.0002998	72	0.0008082	71	0.0012118	66
123 Liberia	–	–	–	–	–	–	4.78 E−08	176	2.06 E−07	170	3.58 E−07	169	7.42 E−07	163
124 New Zealand	0.0032955	52	0.003846	44	0.0029774	48	0.0032656	49	0.0037556	50	0.0054912	53	0.0069998	55
125 Mauritania	–	–	5.26 E−07	131	0.0000024	140	1.61 E−06	147	1.47 E−06	154	4.39 E−06	151	6.04 E−06	149
126 Croatia	–	–	–	–	0.0002484	68	0.0004714	64	0.0006484	62	0.0012106	66	0.000701	74
127 Kuwait	0.0036087	51	0.000995	51	0.0005752	60	0.0008088	59	0.001518	57	0.0045396	54	0.005412	58
128 Moldova	–	–	–	–	1.22 E−06	144	2.17 E−06	144	2.52 E−06	145	8.36 E−06	142	1.18 E−05	143
129 Panama	0.0001533	80	8.05 E−05	81	6.99 E−05	87	0.000106	87	0.0001094	89	0.000187	94	0.0004172	88
130 Georgia	–	–	–	–	8.46 E−07	147	8.79 E−06	131	1.08 E−05	131	3.72 E−05	121	0.0000513	116
131 Bosnia and Herzegovina	–	–	–	–	–	–	2.05 E−05	114	3.88 E−05	108	0.0000868	106	0.0000686	113
132 Puerto Rico	0.0018352	59	0.00166	55	0.0017228	54	0.0023618	51	0.0033244	51	0.0028402	60	0.0022398	63
133 Uruguay	0.0005607	63	0.000171	74	0.0003468	64	0.0004748	63	0.0001445	84	0.000283	86	0.0006138	80
134 Mongolia	7.46 E−05	92	5.06 E−05	91	5.47 E−06	129	1.59 E−06	148	2.30 E−06	147	1.26 E−05	138	3.02 E−05	129
135 Armenia	–	–	–	–	5.91 E−07	149	2.62 E−06	141	5.55 E−06	141	2.72 E−05	127	2.51 E−05	133
136 Albania	3.12 E−05	101	1.65 E−05	106	4.15 E−06	131	7.27 E−06	132	0.0000187	119	4.19 E−05	117	3.41 E−05	126
137 Lithuania	–	–	–	–	8.56 E−06	122	9.09 E−05	89	0.0001956	79	0.0004932	80	0.0004304	87
138 Jamaica	4.59 E−05	97	2.63 E−05	101	3.40 E−05	100	5.53 E−05	97	5.02 E−05	103	5.19 E−05	114	4.43 E−05	122
139 Namibia	–	–	5.74 E−06	120	1.20 E−05	117	0.0000104	127	1.47 E−05	125	2.71 E−05	128	3.40 E−05	128
140 Botswana	8.23 E−06	115	1.95 E−05	105	2.14 E−05	106	2.24 E−05	113	3.09 E−05	112	4.15 E−05	118	4.94 E−05	119
141 Qatar	0.0003522	73	7.58 E−05	83	0.0000697	88	0.0001243	82	0.0004216	69	0.0030666	59	0.007407	54
142 Lesotho	1.19 E−06	125	6.53 E−07	130	1.02 E−06	146	8.08 E−07	154	7.57 E−07	157	1.37 E−06	158	1.56 E−06	160

	value	rank	value	rank	value	rank	value	rank	value	rank	value	rank	value	rank
143 Gambia	6.79 E−07	126	2.72 E−07	135	3.25 E−07	156	0.0000003	162	1.84 E−07	173	2.40 E−07	172	1.71 E−07	174
144 TFYR Macedonia	—	—	—	—	1.06 E−05	120	1.36 E−05	120	1.32 E−05	126	0.0000253	129	2.40 E−05	134
145 Slovenia	—	—	—	—	0.0003242	66	0.00039	68	0.000461	66	0.0007712	72	0.0004938	83
146 Latvia	—	—	—	—	1.29 E−05	115	4.10 E−05	103	8.17 E−05	93	0.0002576	88	0.0001828	99
147 Guinea-Bissau	3.42 E−07	127	1.77 E−07	139	2.55 E−07	159	1.36 E−07	168	1.24 E−07	176	1.94 E−07	173	2.37 E−07	173
148 Gabon	0.0001011	85	5.52 E−05	89	3.90 E−05	98	0.0000246	110	0.0000254	115	5.49 E−05	113	6.43 E−05	114
149 Bahrain	0.0001091	83	4.28 E−05	95	4.42 E−05	94	4.79 E−05	100	0.000076	95	0.0001718	95	0.000211	96
150 Trinidad and Tobago	0.0003412	74	5.59 E−05	88	3.39 E−05	101	3.50 E−05	105	7.46 E−05	97	0.0001584	98	0.0001406	102
151 Swaziland	7.41 E−06	119	2.53 E−06	128	2.99 E−06	137	2.91 E−06	138	2.91 E−06	144	4.44 E−06	150	4.38 E−06	151
152 Estonia	—	—	—	—	4.85 E−06	130	2.40 E−05	111	5.43 E−05	101	0.00014	102	0.0001247	107
153 Mauritius	7.78 E−06	118	9.80 E−06	114	1.47 E−05	112	1.54 E−05	118	1.76 E−05	120	2.39 E−05	130	2.97 E−05	130
154 Timor-Leste	—	—	—	—	—	—	2.72 E−08	180	5.04 E−07	162	4.23 E−06	152	6.26 E−06	148
155 Cyprus	3.52 E−05	100	4.97 E−05	92	0.000074	84	8.46 E−05	90	0.0001148	88	0.0002022	92	0.000127	106
156 Djibouti	—	—	7.32 E−08	145	2.90 E−07	157	2.26 E−07	165	2.22 E−07	169	2.91 E−07	171	4.65 E−07	168
157 Fiji	9.33 E−06	113	3.92 E−06	125	3.45 E−06	134	3.10 E−06	137	2.92 E−06	143	3.54 E−06	154	3.71 E−06	155
158 Equatorial Guinea	1.36 E−08	145	3.72 E−08	151	3.43 E−08	172	4.82 E−07	157	1.27 E−05	128	7.36 E−05	111	0.0000917	109
159 Comoros	1.09 E−07	135	9.97 E−08	142	8.19 E−08	166	3.97 E−08	178	5.25 E−08	181	8.08 E−08	180	8.51 E−08	180
160 Bhutan	1.36 E−07	134	1.44 E−07	140	8.21 E−08	165	1.17 E−07	170	1.92 E−07	171	4.45 E−07	167	7.36 E−07	165
161 Guyana	1.61 E−06	124	1.02 E−06	129	7.68 E−07	148	1.08 E−06	150	8.11 E−07	156	1.16 E−06	160	1.85 E−06	158

(Continued)

IRC, average for periods

Country (ranking according to the number of inhabitants 2017)	1980–1985	Rank	1986–1990	Rank	1991–1995	Rank	1996–2000	Rank	2000–2005	Rank	2006–2010	Rank	2011–2015	Rank
162 Montenegro	—	—	—	—	—	—	1.34 E−07	169	1.59 E−06	151	4.87 E−06	149	4.10 E−06	153
163 Macao	—	—	—	—	—	—	—	—	4.43 E−05	105	0.0001426	101	0.0004654	84
164 Solomon Islands	2.03 E−07	129	6.82 E−08	147	1.22 E−07	163	1.69 E−07	166	7.30 E−08	177	1.08 E−07	179	2.42 E−07	172
165 Luxembourg	0.0001739	78	0.000212	69	0.0003454	65	0.0003426	70	0.000461	66	0.000827	70	0.0007778	73
166 Suriname	1.08 E−05	111	5.76 E−06	119	4.65 E−07	150	1.36 E−06	149	1.47 E−06	153	3.97 E−06	153	5.24 E−06	150
167 Cabo Verde	1.49 E−07	132	1.88 E−07	138	2.24 E−07	160	2.82 E−07	163	4.05 E−07	166	8.23 E−07	164	6.92 E−07	166
168 Malta	7.90 E−06	117	8.28 E−06	115	1.02 E−05	121	1.13 E−05	123	1.52 E−05	124	2.21 E−05	131	2.18 E−05	137
169 Bahamas	3.84 E−05	98	3.60 E−05	96	2.15 E−05	105	0.0000247	109	0.0000275	114	2.14 E−05	132	1.54 E−05	139
170 Maldives	5.35 E−08	141	8.12 E−08	144	1.53 E−07	161	3.90 E−07	161	5.40 E−07	161	1.26 E−06	159	1.66 E−06	159
171 Belize	2.23 E−07	128	2.40 E−07	136	3.69 E−07	153	4.16 E−07	160	5.42 E−07	160	5.74 E−07	165	5.66 E−07	167
172 Iceland	0.000066	94	7.65 E−05	82	0.0000594	93	0.000057	96	7.66 E−05	94	0.0000938	105	5.27 E−05	115
173 Barbados	9.12 E−06	114	8.13 E−06	116	5.55 E−06	127	6.52 E−06	133	6.34 E−06	138	6.66 E−06	145	4.12 E−06	152
174 Vanuatu	9.54 E−08	137	5.45 E−08	149	5.97 E−08	169	5.97 E−08	174	5.55 E−08	180	1.09 E−07	178	1.34 E−07	178
175 Sao Tome and Principe	3.89 E−08	143	3.16 E−08	153	1.64 E−08	173	2.06 E−09	183	5.23 E−09	185	9.73 E−09	185	1.82 E−08	184
176 Samoa	8.40 E−08	138	4.45 E−08	150	4.50 E−08	171	5.87 E−08	175	6.80 E−08	178	1.14 E−07	177	1.34 E−07	177
177 Saint Lucia	1.98 E−07	130	3.38 E−07	134	4.19 E−07	151	4.39 E−07	158	3.80 E−07	167	4.45 E−07	168	3.88 E−07	169
178 Kiribati	9.71 E−09	146	6.22 E−09	154	3.20 E−09	175	3.80 E−09	181	4.26 E−09	186	5.84 E−09	186	7.04 E−09	186
179 St. Vincent & Grenadines	8.29 E−08	139	9.50 E−08	143	1.01 E−07	164	1.12 E−07	171	1.32 E−07	175	1.47 E−07	176	1.09 E−07	179
180 Grenada	1.08 E−07	136	1.35 E−07	141	1.27 E−07	162	1.61 E−07	167	1.91 E−07	172	1.92 E−07	174	1.60 E−07	175

	A		B		C		D		E		F		G	
181 Tonga	4.03 E−08	142	3.53 E−08	152	4.60 E−08	170	3.88 E−08	179	2.70 E−08	183	3.75 E−08	182	4.24 E−08	182
182 Micronesia	—		—		9.40 E−09	174	4.03 E−08	177	3.34 E−08	182	2.40 E−08	183	2.17 E−08	183
183 Seychelles	1.46 E−07	133	1.92 E−07	137	2.58 E−07	158	2.82 E−07	163	3.13 E−07	168	3.11 E−07	170	3.20 E−07	171
184 Antigua and Barbuda	1.94 E−07	131	3.56 E−07	133	3.59 E−07	154	4.37 E−07	159	4.22 E−07	165	5.03 E−07	166	3.27 E−07	170
185 Dominica	5.52 E−08	140	6.86 E−08	146	7.66 E−08	167	8.32 E−08	173	6.79 E−08	179	6.64 E−08	181	5.56E−08	181
186 Saint Kitts and Nevis	3.82E−08	144	6.10E−08	148	7.51E−08	168	1.12E−07	172	1.34E−07	174	1.59E−07	175	1.37E−07	176
187 San Marino	—		—		—		—		6.74E−07	159	1.86E−06	156	7.37E−07	164
188 Palau	—		—		—		3.06E−09	182	1.61E−08	184	1.22E−08	184	1.19E−08	185
189 Nauru	—		—		—		—		1.76E−10	188	4.46E−10	187	2.19E−09	187
190 Tuvalu	—		—		—		2.70E−11	184	1.81E−10	187	2.60E−10	188	3.07E−10	188
Total	100		100		100		100		100		100		100	

2 Global Entrepreneurship – Empowering Diversity and Inclusion in Entrepreneurship

Mirjana Radović-Marković

2.1 Introduction

The future without a doubt belongs to entrepreneurs as a force for positive change. This is something to be really enthusiastic about. However, predicting what will entrepreneurship look like in 10 or 20 years is not an easy task. Therefore, it would be useful for our study to break this question into interrelated questions, such as: What will shape the future of entrepreneurship? Will current entrepreneurs' knowledge and skills be relevant in 5 or more years from now? What future challenges will business owners face? What do entrepreneurs and leaders need to know to work successfully across cultures? Will entrepreneurs of the future be less able to do it alone? Where will the structural changes in the economy and business environment take us? How will entrepreneurship be affected by globalization in small European countries? And finally, how can different modes of action be used to exploit entrepreneurial opportunities in a changeable business environment in the future?

In this context, a prediction is inherently uncertain regardless of the question. Although predictions for the future are bound to be inaccurate, it is worth considering what experts are foreseeing. Namely, their anticipation of future provides some "food for thought" and opens space for new visions.

A large number of studies have been performed over the last 5 years on the various aspects of entrepreneurship (for example, what entrepreneurship is, why entrepreneurship is important, female entrepreneurs' motives, the role of the partner of an entrepreneur, the importance of entrepreneurship education, and so forth) with the aim of developing a better understanding of the underlying mechanisms affecting entrepreneurship. In line with this, researchers are highlighting the importance of new business models within entrepreneurial realms, great diversity of leadership styles worldwide, greater understanding of varying cultures, new funding mechanisms, new ways of organizing business activities, faster delivery of knowledge and accessibility of information across the countries, greater varieties of venture types, as well as an increasing divergence within the workforce.

In order to gain insights into the above-stated questions, recent research has been investigated as well as some main theories. The main objective of our research was to help make judgments about the future of entrepreneurship and also highlight the role of various entrepreneurial perspectives on gender and diversity in organizations.

2.2 Multicultural Business Environment: Challenges and Opportunities

Current trends of the contemporary business world are highly associated with the continuous globalization of the economy. These trends include a growing number of multinational corporations that play an important role in the world economy influencing constant flow of business transactions across countries and increasing divergence within the workforce. Therefore, "understanding the globalisation of business practices is an important area and researchers have been studying the subject of business in multicultural settings for decades" (Ablonczy-Mihályka & Széchenyi, 2009, p. 121).

We live in an era of business without boundaries, where competing effectively means collaborating across time, distance, organization, and culture (Radović-Marković, 2008, p. 4). This process is supported by the "advancements in communications, technology and transportation that have truly made the world a unified global field and have contributed significantly to the globalization process" (Radović-Marković & Vujičić, 2014, p. 53). We are entering a new paradigm called the "Third Wave" of the Internet. The Third Wave of the Internet will transform the economy and the way we do business. It means that entrepreneurs will vastly transform major "real world" sectors like health, education, transportation, energy, and foods (Entrepreneur, 2016). Namely, new technologies have not only made the world a smaller place, but they have altered the nature of work (Radović-Marković, 2008). In other words, they have led together with a new leadership practice to changes in regards to knowledge type and acquiring method (Radović-Marković et al., 2012). At the same time, successfully managing diversity is increasingly recognized as an imperative for the contemporary business world. In this context, global managers should know that diversity not only involves how people perceive themselves, but how they observe others – their gender, ethnic group, age, personality, cognitive style, education, background, and more. Because of new challenges and cyber age, there is a call for a new kind of managing the organizational change (Radović-Marković, 2008, p. 3).

Most recently, a great wave of migrant workers has made a significant impact on organizations in a manner that it requires being open and adaptive toward a different and multicultural working environment. According to a number of scientists, "we should be looking into the concept of an organization and organizational culture rather than a market if we want to understand contemporary economic transformation" (Radović-Marković, 2008, p. 3).

Therefore, managers might find themselves in foreign assignments, managing a workforce that differs in needs and attitude. In line with this, managing global companies pose many opportunities and challenges for the leadership of the company. According to the Harvard Business School, managers can take a quadruple approach to prepare better for managing on a global level. This includes:

1 to develop a clearer understanding of the challenges of managing people across borders;
2 to instill in new global managers an awareness of and an appreciation for the vast differences among the cultures in which they do business;
3 To give global managers the tools and support they need to succeed (Harvard Management Update, 2006); and
4 To acquire new knowledge and a different skill set. Namely, the technologically induced "virtual" environment requires the new work skills and practices (Case, 2016).

2.2.1 *Types of Global Organizations*

The concept of global organization is definitely not new; it has a long history dating back to the 10th century Venetian trading empire. But in recent years, the importance of being global has increased tremendously. It is largely driven by the emerging markets and facilitated by the advancements in communication technology. The increasing trend of globalization is evident by the fact that companies are becoming global earlier in their life cycles. While organizations like Sony and Honda took more than 15 years to become global organizations, Lenovo became a global company in only 5 years.

In examining the different dimensions of globalization, it is helpful to take a look at the various types of global organizations. The global environment contributes to how an organization is established and carries on business. Global organizations are worldwide alliances that imply the partnership of many different countries. These organizations distribute and supply resources to other companies on a global basis in order to provide superior quality product/services at the lowest possible price. Organizations that are global can be categorized into several types based on the location of these companies. The following organizations can be of the three major types: multinational, transnational, and international organizations. Each organization will be explained in full detail and substantial examples of these organizations will coincide.

Multinational companies operate in several countries but manage their company from one main country. These companies are typically stationed with a centralized head office where the coordination of the global management takes place for varying countries. Usually, the company receives a quarter of its income from operations that are outside of its main country. Some examples of multinational companies include Nike, Coca-Cola, Walmart, AOL, Toshiba, Honda, and BMW. Supporters of multinational companies state that they create jobs and wealth by improving technology in countries that are in need of growth. However, critics state that multinational companies can exert an unnecessary political influence on government officials by utilizing developing nations by creating job losses in their home countries.

Unlike multinational companies that manage their company from one main country, a transnational company does not consider any particular country as their main country but rather multiple countries. One of the significant advantages of a transnational company is the ability to maintain a higher amount of responsiveness to the local markets within the area where the facilities are maintained by management. The transnational companies outperform other types of global companies on maturity in development, technology agreements, and the rank of best practice. These organizations combine aspects of the global, multinational, and international companies by balancing out efficiency, maintaining flexibility, and sharing learning and innovations around the world. As organizations continue to mature, flexibility is needed within these companies in order for the processes to be made complete (Martin, 2012).

Transnational companies, like General Electric (Box 2.1), is a top company which contains foreign material goods that are worth $401 billion, which is more than any nonfinancial firm, states the latest

World Investment Report from UN Conference on Trade and Development. Surprisingly, six out of ten of the biggest transnational organizations have foreign resources from oil or power industries.

BOX 2.1 INFORMATION OF GENERAL ELECTRIC

- Founded: April 15, 1892; 126 years ago, in Schenectady, New York, United States
- Founders: Thomas Edison, Charles A. Coffin, Elihu Thomson, Edwin J. Houston, J. P. Morgan
- Headquarters: Boston, Massachusetts, United States
- Area served: Worldwide
- Products: Aircraft engines, electrical distribution, electric motors, energy, finance, gas, health care, lighting, locomotives, oil, software, water, weapons, wind turbines
- Total assets increase: US$ 377.95 billion (2017)
- Number of employees: 313,000 (2017)

Some examples of these foreign companies are Vodafone (Box 2.2), a British telecommunications company, and ArcelorMittal, a steelmaker with its head office in Luxembourg share more than 90% of their total assets (Biggest transnational companies, 2012).

BOX 2.2 HISTORY OF VODAFONE COMPANY

- Public limited company
- Industry: Telecommunications
- Founded
- September 16, 1991; 27 years ago
- Founder: Ernest Harrison, Gary Whent
- Headquarters: London (head office)
- Area served: Worldwide
- Products: Fixed line telephone, mobile phone, broadband, digital television, Internet television
- Revenue: Decrease €46.571 billion (2018)

Lastly, international organizations perform business operations worldwide, but operate in one main country. These international operations include the transfer of goods, services, technology, managerial knowledge, and capital, which export and import their goods and services to other countries. This type of organization has many ways of doing business, which are the following: licensure is given to produce goods within their main country; joint venture is started with a company; branches are opened to produce and distribute goods in main countries; managerial services are provided to companies in main countries; and goods and services are exported to various countries (Akrani, 2011).

International organizations have different features, which keep the organization running smoothly across the globe. Some of the features are the following: integration of economies, domination of developed countries and multinational corporations, participation within countries, competition, and utilization of science and technology. Within large-scale operations, goods are first sold in local markets and then the extra goods are exported to other countries. The integration of economies takes place because the international companies use finance, labor, and infrastructure from different countries.

Many international organizations have expanded their infrastructures and have become top leaders throughout the world. The top three international organizations are Royal Dutch Shell (Box 2.3), ExxonMobil (Box 2.4), and Walmart (Box 2.5). Royal Dutch Shell has increased its earnings through long-term projects like producing gas-to-liquid plants in Qatar and oil sands in Canada. ExxonMobil has increased production by drilling for oil in the Arctic. Walmart has gained profits overseas through their retail distribution of their products (Global 500).

BOX 2.3 KEY FEATURES OF ROYAL DUTCH SHELL COMPANY

- Type: Public limited company
- Industry: Oil and gas
- Founded: April 1907; 111 years ago in London
- Founder: Marcus Samuel, Samuel Samuel
- Headquarters: The Hague, Netherlands (headquarters), Shell Centre, London, England registered office)
- Area served: Worldwide
- Products: Petroleum, natural gas, LNG, lubricants, petrochemicals
- Revenue: Increase US$305.1 billion (2017)

BOX 2.4 INFORMATION OF EXXONMOBIL

- Type: Public
- Industry: Retail
- Founded: July 2, 1962; 56 years ago in Rogers, Arkansas, United States
- Founder: Sam Walton
- Headquarters: Bentonville, Arkansas, United States
- Area served: Worldwide
- Products: Electronics, movies and music, home and furniture, home improvement, clothing, footwear, jewelry, toys, health and beauty, pet supplies, etc.
- Revenue: Increase US$500.34 billion (2018)

BOX 2.5 ABOUT WALMART

- Type: Public
- Industry: Retail
- Founded: July 2, 1962; 56 years ago, in Rogers, Arkansas, United States
- Founder: Sam Walton
- Headquarters: Bentonville, Arkansas, United States
- Area served: Worldwide
- Products: Electronics, Movies and music, Home and furniture, Home improvement, Clothing, Footwear, Jewelry, Toys, Health and beauty, Pet supplies, etc.
- Revenue: Increase US$500.34 billion (2018)

Global companies must focus on three things: to develop a clear understanding of the challenges of managing people across boarders, to instill in new global managers an awareness of and an appreciation for the vast differences of the cultures in which they do business, and to give global managers the tools and support they need to succeed (Rifkin, 2006).

2.2.2 Creating the Culturally Diverse Organization

Globalization can also be viewed from a cultural perspective. Culture is a concept that has gotten much attention in the last couple of years, and a number of studies have been done on culture in different contexts (Holmgren and Jonsson, 2013; Sultana et al., 2013; Radović-Marković, 2014; Ridhi, 2016). The contemporary definition of organizational culture includes what is valued; the leadership style, the language and symbols, the procedures and routines, and the definitions of success that characterizes an organization. The World Commission on Culture and Development noted that a society's culture is "neither static nor unchanging but rather is in a constant state of a flux, influencing and being influenced by other world-views and expressive forms" (UNESCO, 2013). Therefore, "managing in a global environment means you manage people who are separated not only by time and distance but also by cultural, social, and language differences," says Devarajan, managing director of Cisco Systems Global Development Center in Bangalore, India. Cisco India has over 1,500 employees and nearly 3,500 partner employees (Radović-Marković et al., 2014, p. 26). Thus, a culturally diverse workforce must be valued and managed well by all organizations in order to remain competitive in the present global environment. In line with this, managers are faced with the following challenges (Radović-Marković et al., 2014, p. 27):

a   Communication challenges – managers must learn to keep the lines of communication open. Most of the research suggests that an information infrastructure, utilizing modern technology, can support the communication required for effective organization management (Afsarmanesh & Camarinha-Matos, 2005).
b   Frequent communication – it is essential to success.
c   Need appropriate technological support (video teleconferencing, interactive groupware, etc.)
d   Technology challenges – all team members must have the same or similar technologies at their locations.
e   Policies and norms for use must be provided.
f   Diversity challenges – different cultures have different perceptions of time and task importance.
g   Providing the appropriate technologies – the key for each culture.

Globalization has resulted in organizations forming alliances and networks with local, host nations. These alliances are beneficial in that the host country experiences growth but it also helps the organizations save on costs. There are also drawbacks. In addition, there are many tensions between organizations and host countries in the aspect of different values and traditions. Many see the globalization as a way to impose Western opinions and policies. Because of these tensions, international human resource management has become extremely important (Friedman, 2007). They must try to find a balance between the organization's goals and the local culture and customs. Different cultures value different things in the workplace. For example, Chinese managers tend to emphasize office relationships over compensation which is preferred by Western managers (Friedman, 2007). Global managers must choose to develop a reward system that is in line with different national cultures. Performance should be compared across different systems so that there will be a proper evaluation of the skills and effectiveness of managers in different countries. If the global company is a transnational company, which operates in more than one country, then the global manager must decide on whether or not to evaluate employee's performance in the main or overseas country (Dewhurst et al., 2012). In other words, human resources must consider how cultures differ across nations. Cultures that favor long-term orientation honor traditions and prepare for the future. Cultures that value short-term orientation focus on the present. These dimensions show the complications of creating a global organization and merging cultures and traditions. Organizations that do this well are successful in business and in creating benefits for both the employee and the host nation.

2.2.3 *Managing in a Global Environment*

Global diversity must encompass not only an understanding of the differences between different countries, but also, the internal diversity of each country. The scope of diversity has become truly global, and knowledge about each country's customers, employees and suppliers has become essential. The global organizations need to move fast towards better management of a culturally diverse workforce. This movement towards better management has to be adopted by organizations due to three main reasons as illustrated with some real examples. Some companies like Xerox were obliged to develop better management of a workforce made more diverse by affirmative action. Other companies like Hewlett-Packard grew very rapidly and then they realized that they had to work with multicultural constituencies. A third type of company like Avon products needed to have a diverse workforce in order to match the diversity in the marketplace. All these three kinds of companies had to work toward managing their diverse multi-cultural workforce better to gain a competitive advantage in the six dimensions of cost, resource acquisition, creativity, marketing, problem-solving, and system flexibility. Thus, a culturally diverse workforce must be valued and managed well by all organizations in order to remain competitive in the present global scenario. Namely, the global organizations should be able to strike the right balance between the challenges and the benefits of globalization and the four basic areas for striking the right balance are cost, strategy, people, and risk.

Global organizations prosper when they have efficient global managers and leaders. Every leader is confronted with different challenges. Yet, they all function within a diverse environment. Working in diverse backgrounds, leaders must obtain a "global mindset." International managers that practice global mindset are better observers, analyzers, and can detect the best solutions on diverse environments by using reasoning and interactive flexibility. Striking the right balance within a diverse environment can be difficult, but there lies the importance of management and the role of managers and leaders in the organization. There are three critical components of global mindset, which are (a) intellectual capital, (b) psychological capital, and (c) social capital (Rego et al., 2012).

a   The intellectual capital is the skill to comprehend culture, history, geography, and political economic systems worldwide. There are different mechanisms that are associated with intellectual capital as follows: familiarity with the global business, competitors, and industry; knowledge of the global organization and supply chains; the capability to empathize with other people who have different beliefs; and cultural awareness to realize the similarities and differences among other cultures.

b   Psychological capital is having a desire for diversity and self-confidence that help leaders to prosper in foreign countries. Characteristics of psychological capital are resilience, optimism, and self-efficacy in addition to having an optimistic attitude toward other countries and showing interest in other cultures.

c   Social capital is the ability to develop a connection with other countries through intercultural understanding and peacekeeping. The components for social capital are resources resulting from relations by other people in the network.

While global managers lead their companies in a culturally sensitive way, the function of the international business environment is critical to the context of global strategies of the companies. International activities raise issues that arise in more than one country, which deal with stakeholders in foreign countries, including consumers, employees, and governments. The choice of the location and the geographic distribution of activities are notably more complex in an international context due to the variety and diversity of the possibilities that are available. For example, global managers have issues that are present in the international environment like competition, competitive advantage, and pricing strategies that they have to handle differently, depending on the country (Nachum, 2011).

Global managers need to be familiar with the following elements, which are interconnected to the culture: language, legal environment, social setup, material culture, educational system and values, and political environment. Within language, the managers must understand the importance of spoken and written language toward one's own culture. Next, within the legal environment, managers must understand the common laws and regulations, intellectual property laws, and antitrust regulations. In a social setup, the religion must be understood along with the social division of the belief systems, sacred objects, types of prayers, taboos, religious holidays, and social interests. Material culture must be understood through the interventions, scientific achievements, and entrepreneurship in order to understand the risk-taking attitudes and quest to knowledge. The educational system and values must be understood so that attitude toward time, perfection, and completeness can be shown in work. One particular example of a global company that has implemented the global corporate culture into their practice is AT&T. This company has developed a global business curriculum. Within this curriculum, employees are able to learn more about global business training and different areas of study in countries (Admin, 2010).

As globalization evolves, companies must evolve too, and that requires global managers to use their company's global presence to promote worldwide innovation and learning (Churchwell, 2003).

Globalization has led to creating the culturally diverse organization which is characterized by six features as (a) pluralism; (b) full structured integration; (c) integration of informal networks; (d) absence of prejudice; (e) equal identification with goals; and (f) minimal intergroup conflict (Table 2.1).

Table 2.1 Creating the culturally diverse organization

Characteristics	Tools
Pluralism	Training and orientation programs
Full Structural Integration	Education, training, affirmative action, performance appraisal and rewards systems, benefits, work schedules
Integration of Informal Networks	Mentoring, social events, support groups
Absence of Prejudice	Bias-reduction training, focus, task forces
Equal Identification with Goals	Encourage participation of all employees from the diverse workforce in formulating goals, strategies, and mission
Minimal Intergroup conflict	Conflict reduction training, survey feedback

Source: Radović-Marković et al. (2014).

While more complex challenges arise, it is necessary for global companies to make changes because harmony and cooperation within a company help facilitate high performance and success. In this context, managers need to know how leadership is applied in different settings and cultures. However, "many managers do not see the advantages that cultural diversity could bring and how a well managed cultural diversity could essentially achieve competitive edge in the market" (Holmgren and Jonsson, 2013, p. 1). In adddition, a large number of employees that work for the company do not have a desire to learn about the global corporate culture. "This makes the process of developing a global culture challenging for the corporation. It is the use of completing various steps that motivates the employees to build a global corporate culture" (Radović-Marković et al., 2014, p. 13).

Effective leaders create an environment that "encourages involvement, development, and learning from employees" (Rahimi et al., 2011, p. 874). They who want to be successful must be educated to work in a multicultural environment. All leaders who wish to achieve a high level of effectiveness need training in the following:

- Developing a global mind – achieving competence on world issues influencing the organization and the organizations with which it interacts;
- Developing the ability to manage strongly decentralized organizations – there is currently a change in the structure

of international organizations toward a flatter type of hierarchy that consists largely of independently functioning work teams. In this environment the leader's role becomes one of consulting and it departs considerably from the traditional leader's role;
- Developing sensitivity to the diversity issues – the organizational leaders in the modern world need skills for working with groups whose members come from various cultures with different values and worldviews;
- Developing interpersonal skills – the globalized world requires the acquisition and application of salient interpersonal skills for creation of effective interpersonal relations.

Most companies and organizations define and use one preferred leadership model and set of competencies – which is, typically, strongly influenced by Western management theory and practice. However, while Western leadership knowledge and practices have been effective in many parts of the world in the past, this approach has limitations in today's global business environment. In line with this, there is a need for a new vision of leadership as one "based on Eastern, Western, and tribal wisdom."

A greater understanding of differing cultures leads to more positive interactions (Lin, 1999) and more successful business relationships. Different cultures have varying values and philosophies. As a result, certain ideas may have very different connotations for people having different cultural backgrounds. In this context, cultural intelligence is increasingly being considered a critical skill in securing success in the multicultural environment (Ablonczy-Mihályka & Széchenyi, 2009).

The observation that a firm is concerned about diversity in an office is positively correlated with the level of cooperation in that office (Ellison and Mullin, 2014). "Rejecting the cultural differences leads to unproductive working environment which restricts the firm from exploiting its untapped opportunities of its diverse cultural workforce" (Adler and Gundersen, 2008, p. 101).

Beyond management, companies must consider a global strategy with regards to the international business environment. A global business strategy can be defined as the business strategies engaged by the businesses, companies, or firms operating in a global business environment and serving customers throughout the world (Global Business Strategy, 2015). They are developed to meet company's short-term and long-term goals, from day-to-day operations to its future growth, stability, and dominance in its regional and global markets. The difference between a global business strategy and a national business development strategy are the various factors involved, such as standardization, adaptation, and diversification. Each company faces different challenges when determining what their strategy may be, and it is highly dependent on the critical variables of each business and its internal and external environments.

Something else that companies need to look at in terms of their global strategy is global competition. In line with this, a question can be asked: "How should a company build a global presence and then transform this presence into global competitive advantage?" In establishing a global presence, an organization must consider the choice of products, target market groups, and rate of expansion (Brookfield, 2003). To do this, organizations must understand the global market they are entering and establish local advantage. Organizations do this by understanding the culture and the values in these different markets.

Due to the fact that the international business environment is changing at such a rapid pace, customer relations are extremely important. Brookfield (2003) states, "the race will be won, not by those who are big, but by those who are fast." This fast-paced environment requires that organizations have multiple knowledge centers and the ability to foresee the changes before they happen.

2.2.4 Gender and Diversity in Organizations

Advancing gender diversity is a key focus area that organizations should look to, armed with the knowledge that there is still significant progress to make before most workplaces achieve true gender equality (Gorman, 2014, p. 1).

There is not a unique theory of dealing with questions of diversity and gender in organizations. Instead there are many different theoretical approaches and empirical studies. Also, dozens of definitions of the diversity were promoted. The most common definition that researchers use for diversity involves embracing and empowering all minorities. In this context, organizations must adapt to a new business environment and include diversity practices in their small businesses.

Many studies have shown that there are many kinds of discrimination in European countries, which particularly became evident during the economic crisis. The literature review shows that the relationship between marginalized groups and discrimination is not recognized in all countries (Radović-Marković, 2016). For these reasons, there are no proper strategies that will support discriminated people. Marginalization of population can be determined based on a combination of relevant indicators, such as indicators of a high rate of long-term unemployment, low level of education, discrimination, high exposure to health risks, or lack of access to health care (Economic Commission, 2011).

The results of the recent study (Radović-Marković, 2016) showed that education in many countries does not follow the needs of marginalized groups in a sufficient way. Also, on the basis of results gained, it is concluded that the respondents are fully aware that without the appropriate programs adapted to their needs their faster employment cannot be expected, which is one of the basic dimensions of exclusion and poverty. In addition, the respondents did not show the expected interest in self-employment and business start-ups. To get the proper education that would be in function of their employment, a special fund is expected to be established to finance the training of these individuals and monitor the quality of the training programs in accordance with preset standards. Otherwise, education will still not be equally accessible to all, which will result in their exclusion. Respondents also expect that the state should provide more flexible working conditions (working from home, flexible working hours, etc.) as well as to use all mechanisms to protect them from marginalization in employment.

Women represent slightly more than a half of the global population. In many countries, however, limited access to education, labor market conditions, and cultural attitudes are major barriers to workplace entry. There is no consensus among researchers regarding why women remain underrepresented in executive leadership jobs. According to recent research conducted by Organisation for Economic Cooperation and Development, the reduction of 50% in the gender gap in EU member countries could lead to a GDP gain of around 6% by 2030 (Morgan Stanley, 2016).

The most noticeable example of globalization on gender roles can be seen in those countries that give in to global example and begin to promote national equality where there was once extreme inequality.

In December 2015, the European Commission adopted the strategic engagement for gender equality 2016–2019. In this work programme, the Commission has focused on gender equality and women's empowerment. In this work programme, the European Commision (2015) takes into account three types of disadvantages that women are faced with as follows:

- lower hourly earnings;
- working fewer hours in paid jobs; and
- lower employment rates.

The OECD (2016) defines the gender wage gap as "the difference between male and female median wages divided by the male median wages." Gender pay gaps for executives have been smaller in North America than in Europe or the Asia-Pacific, excluding Japan, over the past 10 years (Morgan Stanley, 2016). The extent of the gender wage gap varies from country to country. Namely, the widest gaps are found in Korea where women are paid 35% less than men, and in Japan where they earn 26% less (OECD Observer, 2015). According to statistical data (Eurostat, 2013), average gender pay gap in the EU is 16.3%. The latest ILO report (2016) estimates that women world-wide earn on average 77% of the male wage. In 2015, the average annual salary of a woman was $11,000, compared to $21,000 for a man.

According to recent research done by Gorman (2014),

> organizations that actively manage pay equity vs. making passive commitments ensure that women and men have equal access to profit and loss responsibilities, and proactively support flexible work arrangements driving gender equality at a greater rate than those with traditional diversity programs.
>
> (p. 2)

However, there are still many companies that do not acknowledge that women can do just as good a job as men and there are many limiting sexist and chauvinistic views on women running certain businesses (Radović-Marković, 2009, p. 18).

One group of researchers seems to study diversity from a perspective of investing in gender diversity at the workplace. So, they have shown that multiplier effect of investing in gender equality at the workplace is profitable for both companies and investors (Morgan Stanley, 2016).

A number of researchers have conducted studies in an attempt to explore diversity from an organizational and economical perspective to gain feedback from business leaders on the following (Radović-Marković et al. 2016):

- The career progress;
- Organizational support for women in the senior leadership positions;
- Perceived barriers to the advancement of women into leadership roles.

In line with this, only 5% of global CEO positions are held by women. Beyond this, only 14.2% of the top five leadership positions in S&P 500 companies are represented by females, according to PwC (2016).

A comprehensive analysis of organizational effectiveness has shown that when women reached executive positions, organizations performed better than those who had been managed by men (PwC, 2016). In this context, more women in the senior management roles of a company increases the profitability of a firm (Worstall, 2016). Further, "the positive correlation between the proportion of women in corporate leadership and firm profitability could reflect the existence of discrimination against women executives or the fact that the presence of women contributes to skill diversity" (Noland et al., 2016, p. 3).

There are also multiple theories and observations that are made on the gender gap in senior management positions. There has been also some skepticism about whether women will be able to overcome the obstacles that keep them out of top leadership positions. Namely, despite some progress, women are still significantly underrepresented in the workplace, accounting for an approximately third of all employees globally and less than a quarter of management positions (Morgan Stanley, 2016). In this context, there was conducted an online survey with a sample of 63 respondents to better understand what the barriers are and what the companies are doing to remove them. The research was carried out in Serbia, Italy, Iran, Malaysia, Turkey, India, Denmark, and Portugal. The sample included 63 respondents, among which 39.7% of women and 60.3% of men. Their age was ranging from 24 to 69 years. The survey has shown that 82.5% of the respondents described their title in their company as talent developer and only 17.5% considered their title as nontalent developers. Among respondents, 68.3% were in private and 31.7% were working in public companies. This research shows that the number of women holding senior leadership positions in the companies has changed in the past five years. In other words, the respondents perceive a positive trend in the number of women holding senior leadership positions. Namely, about 36.5% agree that the number of women in senior leadership positions is increased. They also think that 19.9% of women were in the upper management and that their companies continue to create an organizational climate and support the development of women's leaders. Over one-third (36.5%) of the respondents indicated the organizational climate at their companies moderately encourage the development of women leaders (Figure 2.1).

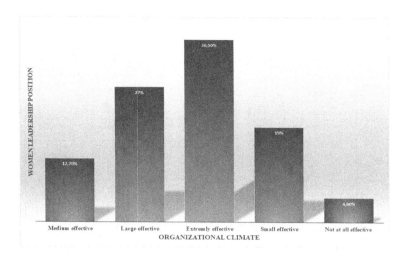

Figure 2.1 Current organizational climate.
Source: Radović-Marković et al. (2016).

Overall, 38.1% of respondents indicated that the development of women leaders within their company was not on the strategic agenda (Figure 2.2).

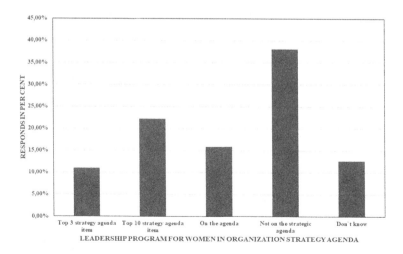

Figure 2.2 Development of women leaders within their company.
Source: Radović-Marković et al. (2016).

The majority of respondents stated that their organizations do not have leadership programs for women (Figure 2.3).

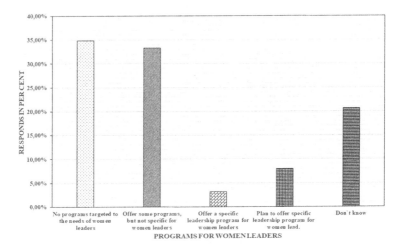

Figure 2.3 Development of women leaders within their company.
Source: Radović-Marković et al. (2016).

Despite the fact that a number of organizations do not have leadership programs for women, one-third or 31.7% of respondents think that there are no barriers in their companies.

Even so, women continue to lag far behind men in senior management positions. In this context, the main reasons why women are still underrepresented in top management are as follows (Figure 2.4.):

a   the existing leadership culture;
b   women are not being in the pipeline long enough;
c   lack of significant general management/line experience;
d   absence of women role models; and
e   lack of leadership programs for women.

Company policies have been responsible for failing initiatives or programs targeted to the needs of women leaders. In addition, the companies are not effective enough in recruiting and training women executives (Radović-Marković et al., 2016).

A number of strategies have been attempted to overcome these barriers. They often adopt models that are outdated and too theoretical to connect with the realities of leadership. Many researchers

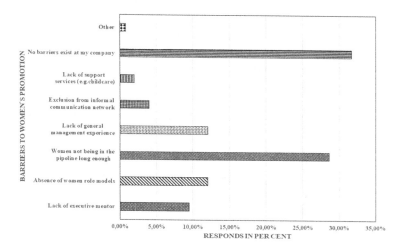

Figure 2.4 The biggest perceived barriers.
Source: Radović-Marković et al. (2016).

have found that more formal bureaucratic organizations with transparent policies can create greater diversity at all organizational levels (Royster, 2003; Wickham et al., 2008). However, the importance of gender diversity goes beyond individual company performance.

In terms of making long-lasting changes, Cortis and Cassar (2005) have suggested that the only way to influence stereotyping and attitudes is to change the culture of management. In addition, "gender discrimination must be demolished in order to bring about true equality and the best conditions in politics, the economy and society as a whole" (Deputy, 2015, p. 20). To overcome existing obstacles and limitations, it is essential to start from attraction of talent as a key planning issue that demands a strategic orientation. In line with this, understanding the talents of a diverse workforce to provide value-added services to a diverse marketplace is imperative for survival and growth. (Madigan, 1997).

2.2.5 *What Will Happen in Entrepreneurship in the Context of Fast-Diversifying Population?*

The future of entrepreneurship will be different from country to country. As stated by Avolio and Radović-Marković (2013), economic, demographic, historical, and cultural differences between countries make the entrepreneurial experiences unique in Europe, Latin America, Central Asia, the United States, and Africa.

Despite these differences, there are common factors that shape the perspectives of entrepreneurship, as follows:

1 **Demographic factors and aging population** – The recent forecasts show that the number of elderly people in the world, those over 60 years, will increase by 39% in the period from 2012 to 2050 (Radović-Marković, 2015). This number will be higher in less developed countries than in more developed ones (66% and 33%, respectively). These trends will make an impact on the type of business and affect its structure. Namely, since people are getting old, they will have different spending and saving models in different phases of their lives.

2 **Increasing number of homepreneurs** – A number of trends and economic shifts make an impact on the growth of home-based businesses (Radović-Marković and Avolio-Allechi, 2013):

Demographic and social shifts – Aging baby boomers, women, and others all view home business ownership as an increasingly important work option. In other words, business chance can be found for the entrepreneurs performing their work at home for the senior citizens, such as healthcare services provision, food preparation, and distribution to old and ill persons, different information and advices provision, etc.

Over the next 20 to 30 years, it is expected that the percentage of people who are self-employed and home-based will be doubled.

3 **Rapid structural changes in the economy and business environment** – It will have an impact on the structure and pace of organization development. Some authors believe that in the future the classical organizational structure will be significantly changed and the team will be the main working unit within the organization.

The criteria for team member selection should include the member character traits. The traits such as vigor, persistence, perseverance, tactfulness, comparability, and loyalty to the firm are the preconditions of team success, as much as the skills and the expertise of the team members.

4 **Continuing trend of development and improvements in Internet and multimedia technologies** – Delivery of knowledge and

information will be faster than now. In line with this, there will be better connections among entrepreneurs wordwide. So, entrepreneurs will be able to get greater ideas and implement them more quickly than ever. In addition, due to new technologies, virtual firms and virtual work will be dominant in the future. In line with this, e-entrepreneurs or popular "digital nomads" will take the important role in the years ahead as a type of entrepreneur. Being a digital nomad means being in a business that virtually has no barriers. It includes pursuing the career of their dreams that they are most passionate about (Taylor, 2016).

5 **Investing in entrepreneurship programs** – Researchers have identified that it is necessary to invest vast amounts of money into entrepreneurship programs by government institutions (Stangler, 2016). Besides government programs, a number of private funds can also attract and accelerate the private sector in the future. Entrepreneurial programs should offer knowledge for detection and analysis of business opportunities. Furthermore, these programs must have a multidisciplinary and process-oriented approach (Radović-Marković, 2015).

6 **Entrepreneurial education** – The new educational programs for entrepreneurs must be based on the exchange of good practice through studying and networking of stategic partners (researchers, entrepreneurs, financiers, policy creators, and others) (Radović-Marković, 2015). They will continue to unleash the entrepreneurial capabilities in the next decade. The entrepreneurial curriculums will be included not only in the schools and faculties of economy but also in the schools and faculties of technical profile, as an important, integral part of their education. It is necessary because the lack of entrepreneurial skills and knowledge would prevent people in their entrepreneurial intentions. Primarily, the support to entrepreneurial activites through entrepreneurial education may contribute to the increase of the number of new companies and to reduction of the level of unemployment. Moreover, education increases the chances of entrepreneurial business success. According to a research, "students with a four-year college degree will earn about $1 million more over the course of their lifetimes than those with just a high-school diploma" (Cohen, 2013).

7 **Resilience of companies for business environmental changes** – Namely, business survival and success in this uncertain

environment demand risk resilience. It means that an organization will be able to anticipate and adapt to change. In this environment, boosting resilience to the risks of economic, social, and environmental shocks will be a top priority.

8 **Management style changes** – Management should not show a passive tolerance for diversity, but must be capable of actively supporting the increasing heterogeneity. In this context, one special area in management is separated, which refers to the cross-cultural organizational management, whose main task is to reveal the ways, methods, and tools for dealing with cross-cultural differences seen as sources of conflicts and misunderstandings in the implementation of joint activity (Jassawalla et al., 2004).

  In the management of virtual intercultural projects, there are two key points that determine the successful operation of this virtual structure: the first point concerns the building of team project manager, which will manage the team, and the second one concerns the building of the virtual team for project management. These two aspects of the implementation of virtuality intercultural projects will be taken into account.

9 **Business networking** – According to researcher Taylor (2016), right networks are becoming currency in this world and especially in the future. Networking through social media is a great way to build up our professional contacts. This future type of networking is crucial to the success of any entrepreneur in any type of business.

10 **Business Strategies for Effective Entrepreneurship** – Global firms will work effectively if they combine a production/service and commercial strategy with technological innovations. Such an approach has enabled them a high competitiveness and a strong position in the global market.

2.3 Conclusion

Over the next decade the ubiquitous digital era will reach its full potential. In line with this, to achieve success multicultural organizations should think and act outside the traditional framework. This implies using new knowledge in the application of the best practical experience, as well as the experience of other organizations which are involved with the same or similar services.

  In order to meet the growing needs of diversity while addressing the issue of globalization, organizations can create effective diversity programs with training at all levels of the organization. By implementing certain policies and training, this keeps both the employees and employers safe from discrimination and allows them the chance to learn about other cultures and start to welcome and accept the differences around the globe.

Managers and supervisors should be encouraged to identify and develop a diverse pool of candidates and develop the people within the organization in order to remain successful and profitable in the global marketplace. However, organizational culture and workforce culture must be compatible. In this context, employees need to view them as equitable, competitive, and appropriate, even though these employees have varied beliefs, values, priorities, and perceptions.

The global corporate culture should focus on the basics of the organization, which includes the vision, values, and behaviors that are essential for the culture. The global vision should be put into action and carried out in an understandable way with acknowledgement of the cultural identity of the different nations. Also, cultural groups must put together forums/meetings in order to distribute awareness and the importance of cultural diversity will make a significant difference.

Global organizations should make an effort to make decisions on a decentralized rather than a centralized basis. Opportunities should be created across the globe and resources should be brought to various locations, so employees can work with different cultures. Lastly, global managers should create culturally sensitive performance reviews and reward systems.

An international organization must develop a set of company ethics to guide employees. It is a challenge for global firms to "manage diversity in order to be more efficient and competitive" (Sultana et al., 2013, p. 133). Corporations must focus on being fast to market, fast to produce, fast to deliver, and fast to service and excite customers.

Studies have shown that creating a positive, diverse culture results in a competitive advantage. This means "better decision making, greater creativity and greater success both internationally and with the local communities" (Sultana et al., 2013, p. 134).

Diversity can be broken into three levels. The first is the internal dimension. The internal dimensions are elements that cannot be changed. Examples are someone's age, race, ethnicity, and sexual orientation. The second dimension is the external dimension. External dimensions can be changed, but individuals are likely to resist changes to this dimension. Examples are someone's education, religion, experiences, and marital status. The final dimension is the organizational dimension. This relates to how someone functions within an organization. These dimensions all interact together and create a corporate culture. Research shows that leadership plays the most important role in defining how groups deal with problems with such diversity.

Ideally, the three rules of cross-cultural leadership include recognizing cultural differences, respecting people's right to differ, and recognizing the issues that the differences create. Leaders and managers might also find that without proper research gender differences might make it difficult to function efficiently. Management practices might need modification to deal with differences in economic values. In this context, managers should identify what type of attitude each staff member is categorized under. According to Gregorie (2017), there are three common characteristics of attitudes when managing employees with diverse backgrounds:

- The first is a parochial attitude, which is the "inability to recognize differences between people." The disadvantage of employees with a parochial attitude is their fellow coworkers may feel that the person is arrogant and disrespectful to their culture, even if the person with the parochial attitude is not arrogant and disrespectful.
- The second is an ethnocentric attitude in which an individual distinguishes that the best method and practice to accomplish tasks are those of their home country. The disadvantage of this attitude is that the person is not open-minded and flexible to adapt to change. Other employees may feel that the person is self-centered. Both of these types of attitudes can affect the cohesiveness of the team, which means less teamwork, motivation to work with certain cultures, and most of all less productivity.
- The third attitude is the geocentric attitude, which "focuses on finding the best approach regardless of its national origin." The geocentric standpoint is the most effective attitude to have, which makes the ideal global perspective work environment.

There are several benefits in having a culturally diverse workforce. Familiarity with different languages and cultures can help in determination of new product lines, service lines, and marketing approaches. It can improve the knowledge base of the manager and improve communication skills of fellow employees. As corporations expand on a global scale, diversity helps speed up the adaptation to new cultures. Ignoring cultural diversity creates tension in the workplace, which leads to conflict and decreased productivity. It may also affect recruiting and retaining employees. Employees, who feel that a violation of their rights occurred, might also initiate legal recourse.

The new management concepts are developed dealing with questions, such as, e.g., organizational learning, multicultural teamwork, gender, and diversity management. Namely, in order to meet the growing needs of diversity while addressing the issue of globalization, organizations should create effective diversity programs with training at all levels of the organization. In addition, organizations that have holistic approaches to support female talents have more comparable talent flows for women and men than those who do not (Gorman, 2014).

Based on her research, Radović-Marković (2008) concluded that "the winners in changeable business environment will be the unbridled firms that are responsive to challenges and adroit in both creating opportunities and capturing them" (p. 3). Also, it is a commitment to foreseeing change, embracing that change, and seeking it constantly.

References

Ablonczy-Mihályka, L., & Széchenyi, I., 2009. Business Communication between People with Different Cultural Backgrounds. *Conference of the International Journal of Arts and Sciences*, 1(19), pp. 121–129.

Adler, N., & Gundersen, A., 2008. *International Dimensions of Organizational Behavior*. 5th ed. Mason, OH: Thomson Learning Inc.

Admin, C., 2010. *Global Organizations: An Analysis*. Software CEO: www.softwareceo.com/search?search=global%20organization [Accessed 26 October 2013].

Afsarmanesh, H., & Camarinha-Matos, L. M., 2005. A Framework for Management of Virtual Organization Breeding Environments. *IFIP — The International Federation for Information Processing Collaborative Networks and Their Breeding Environments*, pp. 35–48. doi:10.1007/0-387-29360-4_4

Akrani, G., 2011, September 9. *What Is International Business? Meaning, Features, and Article*. Kaylan City Life: http://kalyan-city.blogspot.com/2011/09/what-is-international-business-meaning.html [Accessed 27 October 2013].

Avolio Alecchi, B., & Radović Marković, M., 2013. *Women and Entrepreneurship: Female Durability, Persistence and Intuition at work*. Farnham,

UK: Gower Publishing Limited, [2013] xiv, 162 pages str., graf. prikazi, tabele. ISBN: 978-1-4094-6618-5.

Biggest Transnational Companies, 2012. Economist: www.economist.com/blogs/graphicdetail/2012/07/focus-1 [Accessed 30 October 2013].

Brookfield, J., 2003. Globalization and Competitive Advantage. *Strategy and Leadership*, 31(3), pp. 54–55.

Case, S., 2016. *The Third Wave: An Entrepreneur's Vision of the Future*. New York: Simon & Schuster.

Churchwell, C., 2003. *The New Global Business Manager*. HBS Working Knowledge. http://hbswk.hbs.edu/item/3827.html [Accessed 3 August 2015].

Cohen, K., 2013. Why Future Entrepreneurs Should Invest in College Entrepreneur. Available at: www.entrepreneur.com/article/226626

Cortis, R., & Cassar, V., 2005. Perceptions of and about Women as Managers: Investigating Job Involvement, Self-esteem and Attitudes. *Women in Management Review*, 20(3), pp. 149–164.

Deputy, O. M., 2015. *The Evolution of Women in Business and Female Leadership in the Business Environment*. Senior Honors Projects. Paper 129.

Dewhurst, M., Harris, J., & Heywood, S., 2012, June. *The Global Company's Challenge*. McKinsey and Company. www.mckinsey.com/insights/organization/the_global_companys_challenge [Accessed 29 October 2013].

Economic Commission, 2011. *European Economic Forecast*. Brussels: European Union. ISBN: 978-92-79-19317-0.

Ellison, S. F., and Mullin, W. P., 2014, Summer. Diversity, Social Goods Provision, and Performance in the Firm. *Journal of Economics & Management Strategy*, 23(2), pp. 465–481.

Entrepreneur, 2016. How Steve Case Is Preparing for the Web's Third Business Environment Wave. Available at: www.entrepreneur.com/article/275135 [Accessed 5 March 2016].

European Commision, 2015. The Gender Pay Gap in the European Union. Available at http://ec.europa.eu/justice/gender-equality/files/gender_pay_gap/gpg_eu_factsheet_2015_en.pdf [Accessed 15 July 2016].

Eurostat, 2013. Gender pay gap in public services: an initial report. Available at www.world-psi.org/sites/default/files/documents/research/gender_pay_gap_initial_report_may_2013.pdf [Accessed 1 May 2017].

Friedman, B., 2007. Globalization Implications for Human Resource Management Roles. *Journal of Employee Responsibilities and Rights*, 19, pp. 157–171.

Global Business Strategy. Economy Watch. www.economywatch.com/business/global-business-strategy.html [Accessed 03 August 2015].

Gorman, C. (2014). Gender in the Workplace: A Problem That Just Isn't Improving. Available at: www.eremedia.com/tlnt/gender-diversity-in-the-workplace-a-problem-that-just-isnt-improving/ [Accessed 19 July 2016].

Gregoire, M. B. 2017. *Foodservice Organizations: A Managerial and Systems Approach*. Upper Saddle River, NJ: Pearson Education Inc., pp. 112–114.

Harvard Management Update, 2006. Leadership & Managing People [Accessed 18 April 2016].

Holmgren, D., & Jonsson, A., 2013. *Cultural Diversity in Organizations: A Study on the View and Management on Cultural Diversity.* Umeå: Umeå School of Business and Economics.

ILO, 2016. Women at Work: Trends 2016, www.ilo.org/wcmsp5/groups/public/—dgreports/—dcomm/—publ/documents/publication/wcms_457086.pdf

Jassawalla, A., Truglia, C., & Garvey, J., 2004. Cross-Cultural Conflict and Expatriate Manager Adjustment: An Exploratory Study. *Management Decision*, 42(7), pp. 837–849.

Lin, C. Y., 1999. A Comparison of Perceptions about Business Ethics in Four Countries. *Journal of Psychology*, 133(6), pp. 641–655.

Madigan, C. O., 1997. Surveying the Diversity Scene, *Controller Magazine*, May.

Martin, A., 2012. Lessons Learned from Going Global: Two Organization Types Outperform! CedarCrestone: www.cedarcrestone.com/blog/?p=336 [Accessed 26 October 2013].

Morgan Stanley, 2016. Why It Pays to Invest in Gender Diversity. Available at: www.morganstanley.com/ideas/gender-diversity-investment-framework [Accessed 10 July 2016].

Nachum, L., 2011, July 1. International Business Strategy: A Journey of Its Own. *Forbes*: www.forbes.com/sites/85broads/2011/07/01/international-business-strategy-a-journey-of-its-own/ [Accessed 2 June 2015].

Noland, M., Moran, T., & Kotschwar, B. (2016). Is Gender Diversity Profitable? Evidence from a Global Survey. *Working Paper*. Available at: https://piie.com/publications/wp/wp16-3.pdf

OECD, 2016. Gender Pay Gap. Available at: https://data.oecd.org/earnwage/gender-wage-gap.htm

OECD Observer, 2015. No. 302, Q1 2015. Available at: http://oecdobserver.org/news/fullstory.php/aid/4817/Pay_gap.html

PwC, 2016. Spotlight On: Gender Diversity. Available at: www.pwc.com/gx/en/research-insights/spotlight/gender-diversity.html

Radović-Marković, M., 2008. Managing the Organizational Change and Culture in the Age of Globalization. *Journal of Business Economic and Management*, (1), pp. 3–11.

Radović-Marković, M., 2009. Globalization and Gender Participation in the Informal Sector in Developing and Transitional Countries, E + M Ekonomie A Management, 4.

Radović-Marković, M., 2015. Causality among Dual Education, Reducing Unemployment and Entrepreneurial Initiatives of Youth Labour in the Countries of the Western Balkans in Scientific Conference on Leadership and Organization Development, Kiten, Bulgaria, 16–19 June 2016, Sofia University "St. Kliment Ohridski", Faculty of Philosophy.

Radović-Marković, M., 2016. Empowering Employment of Women and Marginalized People through Entrepreneurship Education in Serbia, JWE, 1–2.

Radović-Marković, M., & Avolio-Allechi, B., 2013, September. *Women and Entrepreneurship Female Durability, Persistence and Intuition at Work*. Ashgate, London: Great Britain.

Radović-Marković, M., et al., 2014. *Virtual Organisation and Motivational Business Management*. Maribor: Alma Mater Europea – Evropski Center; Beograd: Institute of Economic Sciences.

Radović-Marković, M., Salamazdeh, A., & Kawamorita Kesim, H., 2016. Barriers to the Advancement of Women into Leadership Positions: A Cross National Study in Scientific Conference on Leadership and Organization Development, Kiten, Bulgaria, 16–19 June 2016, Sofia University "St. Kliment Ohridski", Faculty of Philosophy.

Radović-Markovic, M., Salamzadeh, A., Markovic, D., Grozdanic, R., & Vucekovic, M., 2012, December 1. E-Learning in Business and Entrepreneurship: Evidence from Serbia, Iran, and India. 1st Annual International Conference on Employment, Education and Entrepreneurship, 2012. Available at SSRN: http://ssrn.com/abstract=2203718 [Accessed 5 March 2016].

Radović-Marković M., & Vujičić, S., 2014. *Innovative Global Companies – Some Case Studies in the Proceedings, Lentrepreneurship: Factors Affecting Small-Scale Business Performance and Development*. Belgrade: Faculty of Business Rconomics and Entrepreneurship. http://vspep.edu.rs/_img/downsekcija/2015/08/eeebookofapstracts2014belgrade.pdf [Accessed 20 April 2016].

Rahimi, G., Damirchi, Q., & Seyyeedi, M. (2011). Management Behavior and Organizational Innovation. *Interdisciplinary Journal of Contemporary Research in Business*, 3(6), pp. 874–881.

Rego, A., Pina, M., & Clegg, S. R., 2012. *The Virtues of Leadership: Contemporary Challenges for Global Managers*. Oxford: Oxford University Press, pp. 33–36.

Ridhi, A., 2016. Perspectives of Entrepreneurship and Its Impact on Stakeholders' Co-Creation. In: H. Kaufmann and S. M. Riad Shams (eds.), *Entrepreneurial Challenges in the 21st Century*. Springer, pp. 1–11.

Rifkin, G., 2006. *The Soft Skills of Global Managers*. HBS Working Knowledge. http://hbswk.hbs.edu/archive/5370.html [Accessed 03 August 2015].

Royster, D. A., 2003. *Race and the Invisible Hand: How White Networks Exclude Black Men from Blue-Collar Jobs*. Berkeley, CA: University of California Press.

Stangler, D., 2016. The Future of Entrepreneurship, Innovation Growth Lab. Available at: www.innovationgrowthlab.org/blog/future-entrepreneurship [Accessed 15 July 2016].

Sultana, M., Rashid, M., Mohiuddin, M., & Mohammad, N., 2013. Cross-Cultural Management and Organizational Performance: A Content

Analysis Perspective. *International Journal of Business and Management*, 8(8), pp. 133–146.

Taylor, G., 2016. The Future of Entrepreneurship and Start-ups. Available at: http://gabrielataylor.com/the-future-of-entrepreneurship/

UNESCO, 2013. Culture for Sustainable Development. Available at: www.unesco.org/new/en/culture/themes/culture-and-development/the-future-we-want-the-role-of-culture/globalization-and-culture/ [Accessed 17 May 2017].

Wickham, J., Collins, G., Greco, L., & Browne, J., 2008. Individualization and Equality: Women's Careers and Organizational Form. *Organization*, 15(2), pp. 211–231.

Worstall, T., 2016. Business Gender Diversity Solved: More Women Means More Profits. Available at: www.forbes.com/sites/timworstall/2016/02/10/business-gender-diversity-solved-more-women-means-more-profits/#7b9359bb4b0f

3 Globalization Impact on Entrepreneurship in Small Countries
A Case Study of Serbia

Mirjana Radović-Marković

Introduction

The contemporary business world is connected to continuous globalization of economy. This trend includes an increasing number of international corporations, increase in the power of global economic competition, definition of new types of business, change of business structure and leadership styles, and effect of the increasing diversity within labor. Globalization has also affected small and medium companies by changing their role, primarily, in national economies. In addition, globalization offers the possibility SME to take part in regional and international market, while internationalization is a possibility for growth even out of the local framework (Seila, 2014).

Critics and opponents of globalization insist on its negative effects, stating that:

- Globalization brings benefits only to economically developed countries,
- International financial institutions instead of encouragement interrupt economic development of developing countries,
- The gap between rich and poor is continuously growing.

Negativist attitude toward globalization very often gets wide proportions. Such attitudes have led to big debates, which tried to confirm or deny who will gain most benefits – developed or undeveloped countries, small or big countries in conditions of new economic movements under the impact of globalization. However, the thing that cannot be the subject of any dispute and that majority of economic experts agree with is the fact that mutually connected economic, political, cultural, and institutional dimensions of globalization cannot easily be separated from each other.

In addition, there is a general consent regarding the most important aspects of globalization (Radović-Marković, 2018a):

- Globalization has led to an increased number of new jobs and thus the increased employment. The economists agree that in the United States there was created more than 50% of new jobs in the last decade which is directly related to global economy;
- New technologies have become a crucial business factor and a significant competitive advantage of companies in contemporary business conditions. Using technological advantages, especially in domain of information and communication technologies, has the impact on a closer connection of economies in time and space making those jobs performed in a new manner and through a closer mutual interaction. There are also introduced new communication and coordination systems, as a link between different organizational cultures;
- New organizational culture of companies is created under the impact of global movements;
- Globalization gives an opportunity of a greater cooperation between suppliers, manufacturers, and buyers and enables a much more fluid marketing environment where an organization can extend its markets and thus increase its gain;
- There has come an integration of financial markets. Namely, globalization affects the financial sector to a greater extent in relation to other sectors since money transfer is performed through computer operations. Having this in mind, it is not surprising that this sector has not experienced the impact of globalization;
- Globalization has largely reflected itself on the change of the trade structure and increase of foreign direct investments and competitive advantages of some countries;
- International economic institutions such as the World Trade Organization (WTO) and International Monetary Fund (IMF) advocate for reduction of barriers in case of the flow of goods, services, and money at an international level. At the regional level in similar manner, they advocate the European Union (EU), Association of South-Eastern Asian Nations (ASEAN), and North American Free Trade Agreement (NAFTA);
- Globalization promotes relocation of companies and movement of business that abroad have additional elements of reducing business costs;
- Appearance of new economy – which refers to interaction between globalization and "knowledge society" – increasingly

transforms traditional economic competition into technological competition;

- Globalization affects to follow strategy of the company more than ever, which today implies multifunctional teams led by older managers, who do not travel throughout the world their whole life closing the deals, but communicate electronically with virtual teams throughout the planet. That is the explanation why globalization can never be related only to business with one region or market. According to that, global companies are distinguished by their possibilities not only to serve a great number of markets but to use all market possibilities and increase their competitive advantages.

Shortly, the globalization concept essentially includes the idea of the integration of national economic, financial, and market activities (Lee & Vivarelli, 2006). This process supports "progress in communication, technology and transport" (Radović-Marković & Vujičić, 2014, p. 53). The latest phase of globalization is determined by the following crucial characteristics: (a) integration of big markets; (b) new business models, and (c) increased mobility of resources over borders. Based on this, we will set the basic hypothesis of the research we want to prove.

- Hypotheses

H0. Level of total entrepreneurial activity (measured by global entrepreneurship index) in the country is positive in relation to a country's globalization level (measured by KOF) (Incekara & Savrul, 2012).

H1. As the country is more globally integrated, it is more resistant to negative encouragements from global business environment (Petrylė, 2016).

H2. The most efficient manner for the increase of resilience of some organization is a strong system of motivation, which encourages the individual to learn, develop, and adapt to their own environment (Southwick et al., 2014).

H3. The main obstacles to the successful implementation of the business continuity in small and medium enterprises is the lack of action plans and understanding of the importance of business continuity (Heng & Wong, 2015).

H4. Owners of small businesses have little awareness of the importance of insurance to encourage the resilience of small and medium-sized enterprises (Chatterjee & Wehrhahn, 2017).

3.1 Literature Overview

The latest empirical studies point to the multidimensionality of globalization. In addition, there are offered new methods in access to globalization (Dreher, 2006; Ursprung, 2006; Gemmell et al., 2008). Their methods are based on two theories: (1) theory of efficiency and (2) compensation theory. In efficiency theory, globalization of economy reduces state outcomes and in some economic conditions, state and private sectors are equalized. In compensation theory, globalization of economy carries along certain risks for the society and national economy (Sadeghi & Sameti, 2012). Compensation theory is also supported by well-known economist and Nobel Prize winner Stiglitz (2003), considering that globalization has led to a clearly expressed need for a new type of social, political, economic regulation and different activities of the states. Stiglitz stresses that governments can reduce the risk and improve the outcome of globalization impact through well-selected intervention measures.

Having in mind that globalization is a phenomenon that has an impact on economy, causing positive and negative consequences, it is best to put this analysis in the context of small economies due to their specificities as follows:

- Great sensitivity of small countries to external impacts: Small economies are particularly susceptible to external impacts, including natural disasters, which cause high volatility in national income;
- Small diversification of economy: When one dominant economic activity decreases, it is being replaced by another. They are also oriented on a small number of export destinations (Lederman & Lesniak, 2017). It increased the vulnerability of economy of small economies to changes in external environment;
  - Higher level of poverty and inequality: the studies show that in small countries there is a higher level of poverty and higher inequality in allocation of earnings that in big countries (World Bank, 2000).
  - Insufficient institutional capacities: Faced with challenges and possibilities of globalization, small countries cannot entirely take part in international finances and trade agreements due to unfavorable institutional capacities, which can have a negative impact on their economies.
  - Less availability of global capital market: Access to external capital is important for small countries and it represents one

of the manners to compensate for income instability. However, investors have the tendency to see small countries as risky areas in relation to bigger countries, and thus their access to global market is more difficult.

- Higher transport costs: Small economies also pay higher transport costs due to small cargo units, which increase export costs and reduces their competitiveness. At the same time, import costs are increased.

In spite of the fact that size of a country can also have many implications for development of the same, it is important to mention that small size does not necessarily have to lead to lower growth rates or development level. From the characteristics mentioned, trade and investments are the key of small economies, which can help them overcome all constraints of size.

Although in literature we can find the opinions of a number of economists that small countries have a tendency to equally react to risks and possibilities of globalization (Lindert & Williamson, 2001), studies have shown that they are mutually different in this aspect. This was contributed by their different development histories and development strategies, which have affected the formation of different groups of institutions. On them precisely to the greatest extent depends how the globalization performs the impact on each country (Bräutigam & Woolcock, 2001). According to the studies of Bräutigam and Woolcock, small European countries are open for international markets of goods, people, and ideas and they are better integrated in global business flows than big countries. Primarily, small countries can succeed in globalization processes if they are able to increase economic competition and innovations and simultaneously reduce the poverty, illiteracy, unemployment, and social violence. In addition, small countries with macroeconomic stability will easily attract direct investments and they will rapidly integrate themselves into global processes. Small developed countries such as Singapore, Switzerland, the Netherlands, or Baltic countries have been a good barometer of the functioning of global economic system (Skilling, 2012).

Globalization impact on development of entrepreneurship is the subject of the analysis of many studies (Knight, 2000; Sakai, 2002; Milner & Kubota, 2005). According to Knight (2001), the more a company is integrated in global business flows, the better are its performances. A great number of scientific papers refers to the creation of encouraging business environment, which enable the enterprises the easiness of business and guarantees the entrepreneurs and financiers that their rights and contracts will be respected (Beck et al., 2005). These analyses of business environment have shown, among other things, that a less bureaucratized business environment is favorable for the development of entrepreneurial sector and economic development of small countries (Altenburg & Drachenfels, 2008).

Many authors stress the importance of innovations, learning, networking, and internationalization of small and medium enterprises (Atristain & Rajagopal, 2010; Campaniaris et al., 2010; Awuah & Amal, 2011). "We can say that SME organization – particularly networking, information and communication technologies, innovations and their implementation are basically a precondition for the achievement of their success in the new world of globalization" (Lesáková, 2014, p. 114). Networking enables small and medium companies to combine advantages of smaller scope and greater flexibility with economy of scope and economy of extension on greater markets – regional, national, and global. There are formed alliances of organization, which integrate business processes of different organizations in order to adapt themselves to the business environment in a global market. As a result, SME become more and more included in international relations through strategic alliances and common investments (Smolková, 2010).

All the waves of globalization in modern history were in one way or another encouraged by technical and technological innovations that reflected itself on the change of business in a fundamental manner. Namely, of extreme importance is the development of information and communication technologies, which pressure the small companies to look for new, flexible, and efficient forms of organization. Namely, in accordance with these changes, enterprises look for new models of organizational relations that suit more to the existing business environment, stressing the development in two complementary directions:

1   Modification of organizational structure that will enable rapid adaptation to the altered business conditions, both in the market and within borders of the enterprise itself, with minimum costs and with as high a product quality as possible (Pollalis & Dimitriou, 2008); and
2   Intensive usage of information communication tools for information and knowledge management.

Special forms of networking, suitable for SME, are virtual organizations. The concept of a virtual company meets the answer to the two abovementioned requirements (Iandoli et al., 2014).

Virtual enterprises appear in the market as independent entities, in spite of their internal modular units and open organizational structure. Organizations that initiate the cooperation thus determine the most favorable business processes that are complementary to the business skills of different companies.

Development perspectives of virtual organizations are in literature considered dually as:

- *structural perspectives* – focused on construction of clusters of virtual companies and their features
- *process perspectives* – oriented on organizational behavior and work

In case of this organizational form of enterprise, for its success it takes more than relying on contemporary technologies. First of all, it takes good strategies and communication, as well as good management with them.

The example of using the globalization possibilities for SME development offers (especially in countries with small internal market), global start-up companies. Namely, talking about the future of entrepreneurship sector, a great number of researchers in the world believe that global start-ups will change global business and business style (Lesáková, 2014; Devinney et al. 2016). It is about an organization that extended itself to more than 15 countries and achieves more than a billion of USD annual income. Global start-up companies play an important role in development of innovations. They are formed to exploit the possibility in the international market in almost every sector. Although small and medium companies are traditionally thought to be endangered in internationalization due to limited size and resources, they play an important role in this type of internationalization.

Innovations in economic literature are often related to the survival of enterprise in the global market (Audretsch, 1991; Helmer & Rogers, 2008). These studies conclude that enterprises that more rapidly adopt the innovations are the ones that more frequently survive. From this standpoint, it is concluded that patents are closely related to a company's productivity (Bloom & Van Reenen, 2002; Klette & Kortum, 2004). Thus, we can expect for the companies that use more patents to be in greater extent innovative and to, accordingly, be in advantage in relation to their competition (Helmer & Rogers, 2008).

The latest studies of globalization process are mainly based on determination of integration level of particular countries, based on the two principles:

1 determination of globalization index and
2 determination of attractiveness of the country for foreign investments. In this chapter, we have performed the study of positioning of Serbia and Western Balkan countries on these principles, as well as their relevance in the global economic framework.

3.2 Macroeconomic Environment in Serbia and Western Balkan Countries – GDP Growth Movement

In the period between 2006 and 2016, gross domestic product (GDP) of Serbia has achieved an average growth of 1.3% (Eurostat, 2017). Based on reports of Republican Bureau of Statistics, real growth of GDP in Serbia in the second quarter of 2017 was 1.2% greater in relation to the same quarter in 2016 (Republican Bureau of Statistics, 2017).

Differences in increase of GDP, observed for Western Balkan countries in the period 2006–2016, are not drastic (Figure 3.1). They move at the average level for the entire observed ten-year period

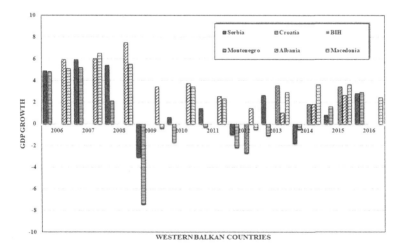

Figure 3.1 GDP growth, 2006–2016 (%).
Source: Author according to the data taken from Eurostat, 2017.

from 1.3% in Serbia to 3.3% in Albania. Croatia is the only one that recorded a negative growth rate of −0.2% for the same analyzed period (Eurostat, 2017).

The data on achieved level of GDP for the period 2006–2016 point out that Western Balkan countries have a rather harmonized development level (Figure 3.2).

Analysis of GDP per capita for small countries in Europe (Table 3.1) are especially used in our study due to determination of their correlation with globalization index.

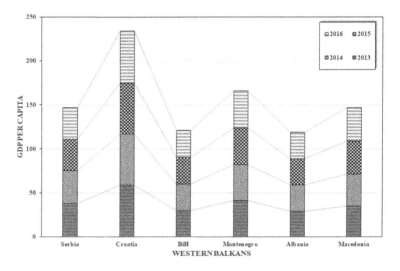

Figure 3.2 GDP per capita 2013–2016.
Source: Author according to data taken from Eurostat, 2017.

Table 3.1 GDP per capita for small European countries

Country	Population in mil.	GDP per capita
Serbia	7.10	$12,893
Croatia	4.2	$20,063
Montenegro	0.6	$14,152
Macedonia	2.1	$12,609
B&H	3.8	$9,387
Albania	2.9	$10,405
Bulgaria	7.2	$15,695
Cyprus	1.2	$27,394
Czech Republic	5.6	$41,991

Country	Population in mil.	GDP per capita
Estonia	1.3	$25,132
Finland	5.5	$38,846
Georgia	4.5	$6,946
Hungary	9.9	$22,914
Iceland	0.3	$41,250
Ireland	4.6	$44,931
Latvia	2	$21,825
Lithuania	2.9	$24,483
Luxembourg	0.6	$87,737
Moldavia	3.6	$4,521
Norway	5.1	$62,448
Slovakia	5.4	$26,263
Slovenia	2.1	$27,576
Sweden	9.7	$43,741
Switzerland	8.2	$54,697
Austria	8.5	$44,376

Source: Author.

3.3 Impact of Globalization on Competitiveness

With the change of business environment and under the impact of globalization, small economies have particularly faced numerous challenges, such as the issues of international competition (Ruzzier et al., 2006). As a result of entering the global market, competition raises the quality of products, increases the scope of available products and services, and raises prices at lower level (Lee & Carter, 2005). However, extension of the market does not mean that only big business subjects will be able to gain benefits from this trend. Studies have shown that there is no correlation between big market and success of big businesses. In other worlds, globalization rewards the companies that are innovative and competitive, regardless of the size of organization and country of origin.

Western Balkan countries, which strive to integration in EU and exit from domestic enterprises and economy to European and global market, are ready to change business strategies in order to achieve competitive advantage. This implies observation of organization such as a system, which make mutually intertwined many functions and characteristics. They determine business success of the given organization. Companies, which are not treated in that way do not manage to adapt themselves to new requirements and thus they are in danger to lose their strategic advantages. However, those companies that easily adapt to new organizational requirements increase their strategic maneuvering space and thus create additional competitive possibilities in the market. Competitive advantage of the enterprise must not be increased only by the reduction of costs but also through the achievement of high quality of production, continuous development of products and services, comprehensive concept of services, or ability to rapidly respond to the requirements of buyers and business partners.

The transition process in Serbia was since 2001 followed by a series of adaptations and accelerated harmonization of economic policy and new economic order. The program of Serbian reforms was, among other things, oriented on revival of economic growth through reorientation of a country from the economy based on social ownership to the economy with an increased share of private sector. In accordance, Serbia has followed EU by reducing the backlog in development of private sector in relation to EU member countries and developed SME sector. According to that, the Serbian government in March 2015 has adopted the strategy for support to development of SME, entrepreneurship, and competitiveness for the period from 2015 to 2020 in order to improve the development of entrepreneurship, increase the number of small and medium companies, increase employment and train SME to answer the increasing pressure of competition in the market. If the competitiveness in global market is weak, then national economy suffers as well, which leads to protectionism, nontransparent state grants, and barriers for entering the market (Federal Bureau for Development Programming of B&H, 2012).

3.3.1 Global Competition Index – GCI

Global Competition Index – GCI analyzes the factors that lead to productivity and prosperity. It is about a rather comprehensive index, which includes micro and macroeconomic bases of national competitiveness. GCI results are calculated with the help of data that cover 12 pillars: institutions, infrastructure, macroeconomic environment, health and elementary education, high education and professional training, efficiency of goods market, efficiency of labor market, financial market development, technological readiness, market size, business sophistication, and innovativeness. According to the definition, the higher the competitiveness level of a country is, the higher is its productivity, which should lead to greater and more sustainable economic growth (Petrylė, 2016).

Although the global competitiveness index in Serbia has had significant fluctuations in the last couple of years, it mainly increased in the period from 2007 to 2016, in order to have the best ranking improvement (by 12 positions) in 2017 (Table 3.2). Albania has, in addition to Serbia, had the greatest increase of its position, i.e., from the 93rd position in 2016 to 80th in 2017. The other countries from the region had a rank improvement in 2017 in relation to the previous year, while Croatia has occupied the same position as in 2016.

Comparing the Western Balkan countries with developed European countries in the aspect of their competitiveness, it is observed that they have significantly reduced backlog and the existing difference from the EU countries. For this backlog to be reduced, Serbia has managed to significantly improve its business primarily due to economic reforms. Primarily, labor law has enabled easier employment and dismissal of employees. In addition, economic growth is a consequence of a lower level of budget deficit, growth of credit rating of a country, and lower level of public debt expressed in GDP.

3.3.2 Attractiveness of Serbia and Western Balkan Countries for Foreign Investments

Determination of impact of globalization to the economy of some country especially puts the stress on its attractiveness for foreign investments and attraction of foreign direct investments. According to the data of the National Bank of Serbia (2017), in Serbia there

Table 3.2 GCI for Western Balkan countries

Country	GCI 2015–2016		GCI 2016–2017	
	Value	Rank	Value	Rank
Serbia	3.97	90	4.14	78
Macedonia[1]	4.23	60	–	
B&H	3.80	107	3.87	103
Albania	4.06	93	4.18	80
Montenegro	4.05	82	4.15	77
Croatia	415	74	4.19	74

Source: Schwab (2016), The Global Competitiveness Report, 2016–2017 and 2017–2018, World Economic Forum.

[1] Macedonia was not included due to lack of data for 2017.

were foreign investments in the amount of 1.9 billion EUR in 2016. Investors find the stability of a country they invest to be rather important, so the continuity is the most important fact when choosing a country they will invest financial funds into. According to that, we can find the explanation why there was greater interest of investors for Serbia. Primarily, it is a result of the positive trend of macroeconomic stability, inflation rate which is below the target level in recent years, drop of budgetary deficit, stopping public debt from growing and stability of exchange rate. In addition, the reasons must be sought in political stability of a country as well. All of this together has affected the growth of confidence of foreign investors in the economic system of Serbia, especially those countries that want to expand their influence in this part of Europe.

The new Silk Road or the Belt and Road should reconnect the continents, joining the East and the West, and for this purpose, the construction of high-speed railways, new ports, technological parks, and a network of highways in the length of 13,000 km is planned. The "one-way one-way" strategy was launched informally in 2011, when the first 11,179 km long railway line linked China's Chungking to Duisburg in Germany.

China is among those countries which are interested in expanding their influence in the Western Balkans. Namely, "Chinese view the region as a gateway to the European Union market and as a land bridge between the Chinese-owned port of Piraeus and Central Europe" (Hänsel & Feyerabend, 2018, p. 6). Thus, China has begun to increase bilateral trade with the countries of the region and is investing in developing the transport and energy infrastructure and in certain strategic industries in the Western Balkans. For these reasons, China has signed a large number of bilateral agreements with Serbia, "agreed on $3 billion package of economic investments" (BIRN, 2018). However, Chinese investments in Serbia with current and announced projects should reach $ 10 billion in 2019.

The result of strong bilateral links between two countries can be recognized in a number of projects over the past few years. Chinese build highways, railways, bridges, energy, and other infrastructure facilities, as well as factories and the construction of large industrial–technological parks in Serbia. One of the greatest Chinese investments in Serbian economy was in "Železara Smederevo." In addition, China has invested in traffic infrastructure starting with the construction of the "Pupin Bridge" in Belgrade, then in building of the highways part of the Pan-European Corridors X and the so-called Corridor XI that connects Serbia with Montenegro. It is a great opportunity for Serbia to improve its railway infrastructure, which has already begun with an agreement on the improvement of the Belgrade–Budapest line. Construction of the Belgrade–Budapest railway line clearly show intentions to build a unique transport system so that goods from China can be transported from the port of Piraeus to Central Europe and vice versa.

Also, Chinese company Zijin has become the strategic partner of RTB Bor, and Huawei Technologies will upgrade the Serbian phone company. Therefore, the investment of 1.26 billion dollars and 200 million for the settlement of debts of RTB was the largest investment in 2018 in Serbia. The Chinese will invest $ 1.26 billion in RTB in the next six years, of which 75% will be invested in the first three years.

The Chinese build a new 350 MW power block in the Kostolac thermal power plant, the largest investment in the domestic energy sector and the first large power plant that is being built in Serbia after nearly three decades.

The total value of the second phase of the modernization project of TPP Kostolac B is $ 715.6 million, of which the investments in the construction of the new block B3 of 350 MW is $ 613 million. Chinese loans for major infrastructure projects are mostly provided by the China Exim Bank.

In a short period of time, China more than doubled trade with Serbia, but export from Serbia is still very small (Figure 3.3).

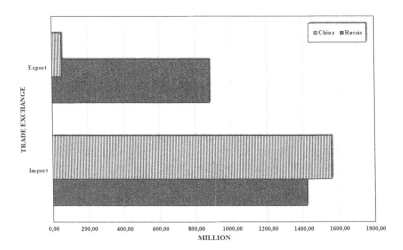

Figure 3.3 Import and Export with China and Russia, 2017.
Source: Author.

How much will the Chinese investments contribute to Serbia's economic development and how much to Chinese ambitions in Western Balkans as well as their political consequences, opened a debate among scholars and politicians. They are divided into those that are against China's influence in the Western Balkans and those who think that it will generate economic opportunities and challenges for the region. Despite their different views on strengthening the influence of China among the Balkan countries and possible long-term political consequences, recent research findings of Le Corre and Vuksanovic (2019) has shown that "Serbia seems focused on the recovery of their own country rather than geopolitics." It is confirmed with

> the last key conclusion for EU institutions emerged from examining the Chinese approach to Serbia, especially regarding aid and investment, and that is that money has flowed for activities which Belgrade thought were in its best interest, rather than priorities that the Chinese determined from Beijing.
>
> (AFET, 2017, p. 43)

Since the 19th century, Russia has developed historical relations with Serbia and the states of the region. In line with this, there are close ties between all the Western Balkan states and Russia. "This reality has allowed Serbia the leeway to play its non-aligned card, delicately balancing off powers against each other so long as the areas of interest do not overlap" (AFET, 2017, p. 45).

Russia has expanded its involvement in the Serbian economy through not only corporate investment but also via direct government-to-government loans. According to data, Russia's economic involvement in Serbia is about 10%, concentrated mainly in the energy sector and banking (European Western Balkans, 2018). In 2016, Russia was the 9th largest investor in Serbia, with EUR 81.2 million worth of investment (AFET, 2017, p. 34). Also, the Russian Federation is Serbia's second largest trading partner which has benefited from reduced trade barriers (Figure 3.3). The agreement stipulates that goods produced in Serbia – meaning those products which have at least 51% value added in the country – are considered of Serbian origin and are exported to Russian Federation customs free.

Despite China playing an increasingly active role in Serbia and traditionally close cooperation with Russia, Serbia is not abandoning the European path. So, trade and investment in Serbia is dominated by EU states. Much as with trade, the EU is the single largest investor in the Serbian economy, accounting for approximately about 85% of FDI in the first half of 2017 (National Bank of Serbia, 2017).

Growth of foreign investments can clearly be seen in the increase of employment of domestic labor. Thus, in comparison to June 2016, total registered employment in Serbia is greater by 2.7% or 54,240 people. In case of legal entities, the number of employees was increased by 34,388 people, while in case of entrepreneurs by 18,648 people (Republican Bureau of Statistics, 2017).

The inflow of foreign direct investments in B&H in 2016 was 536.3 million CM (Central Bank of Bosnia and Herzegovina, 2017), while in FYR Macedonia, foreign investments have reached 105.7 million EUR (in the first quarter 2017) in spite of political crisis in the country.

FYR Macedonia has made great steps in the last couple of years in the aspect of improving business environment and all of that in order to attract foreign direct investments. It resulted by its better positioning toward Doing Business list (2017) in relation to other Western Balkan countries.

The increase of foreign investments in B&H of 28.7% in relation to the same period 2016 encourages the fact that having in mind that in recent years there was a drop in value of foreign investments. It is expected that this trend will continue in B&H, having in mind that competent institutions intensively work on promotion of the country and the possibilities for investment. According to the data of the Central Bank of Montenegro, total inflow of foreign direct investments in the first six months of this year was 273.8 million EUR, which is the result of adoption of legal and operating framework according to the EU norms (CDM, 2017).

Slow progress in reform of business climate in Albania had a crucial importance for the attraction of foreign investments from 2010–2015. However, the greatest progress is noticed in 2016 in relation to the previous period when foreign direct investments in Albania had reached 983 million EUR. In relation to 2015, it is an increase of 10.5% according to the latest report of Central Bank of Albania (Međak, 2018).

3.4 Research Methodology

Scientists and experts of economics have looked at the concept and process of globalization from various viewpoints, including whether globalization causes a higher gross domestic product (GDP) and economic growth. This research is based on an overview of references and statistical data (KOF globalization index for the measurement of globalization level, global entrepreneurship index, global resilience index), both as own latest studies (2015–2017).

In order to examine the hypotheses set, the study was initiated by determination of causality between GDP per capita and index of globalization (KOF). It should be clear that globalization affects economic growth in small countries differently.

With the intention to have a higher precision of the results obtained, small countries were divided into three groups:

a   those that have GDP per capita below 25,000 US $
b   those that have GDP per capita between 25,000 US$ and 50,000US$
c   those that have GDP per capita overt 50,000 US $

3.5 Research Results and Discussion

*   *Impact of globalization (measured by index of globalization) on GDP per capita for small countries*

Results obtained in our research for small countries with GDP below 25,000 US $ per capita indicate that there is a positive but moderate relationship between the variables economic growth and index of globalization ($R^2 = 0.5395$) (Figure 3.4).

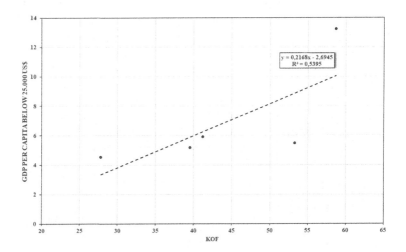

Figure 3.4 Impact of globalization (measured by index of globalization) on GDP per capita for small countries (GDP per capita below 25.000 US $).

Source: Author.

These countries are not highly developed and not well connected to global markets. The reason is that low-ranking nations opened themselves to the world economy later than more industrialized countries, and that some still face barriers to trade and market entry. This implies that if countries which are found in this group want a greater economic growth, they have managed globalization well. Stiglitz (2003) explained that globalization could be either a success or failure, depending on its management. So, relationship between economic globalization and economic growth could be changed by the set of complementary policies. In line with this, globalization by itself does not increase or decrease economic growth. "The effect of complementary policies is very important as it helps countries to be successful in globalization process" (Samimi & Jenatabadi, 2014, p. 2).

This research shows that the mentioned correlation is the strongest for small countries that have GDP per capita between 25,000 US$ and 50,000US$, i.e., $R^2 = 0.8736$ (Figure 3.5). Because they are acutely exposed to the global economy and well-integrated into global market, they have resulted in an increase of real GDP per capita. It explains that globalization is strongly tied to the economy.

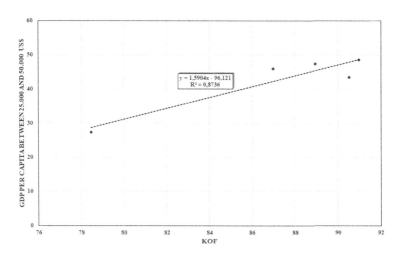

Figure 3.5 Impact of globalization (measured by globalization index) on GDP per capita for small countries (GDP per capita between 25.000 US $ and 50.000 US $).

Source: Author.

On the other side, the weakest correlation between variables is for countries that have GDP per capita over 50,000 US $ (R^2 = 0.3739) (Figure 3.6). Empirical evidence suggests that these countries were sufficiently rich when it comes to globalization (Kuepper, 2018).

Comparing index of globalization among Western Balkan countries (Table 3.3), we observe a great gap between Croatia (the best ranked, i.e., 24th place) and other countries in this region (e.g., FYR Macedonia is at the 94th place).

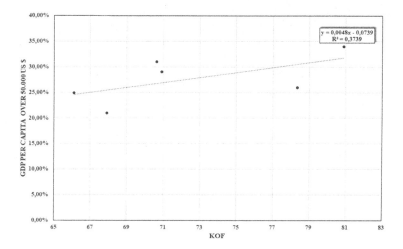

Figure 3.6 Impact of globalization (measured by globalization index) on GDP per capita for small countries (GDP per capita 50.000 US $).

Table 3.3 Index of globalization in Western Balkan countries

Country	Index of globalization	Rank
Croatia	81	24
Serbia	69	46
Macedonia	55	94
Montenegro	65	63
Bosnia and Herzegovina	66	57
Albania	60	76

Source: KOF Index of Globalisation (2017).

3.6 Impact of Globalization on Entrepreneurship Development in Western Balkan Countries

Global Entrepreneurship and Development Index, GEI (Acs et al., 2017), is an indicator of entrepreneurship quality, especially related to entrepreneurship and innovations effects, which are conditioned by individual and institutional factors. GEI measures the intensity of the impact of different factors on entrepreneurship development in the country. GEI contains of three subindexes: (1) entrepreneurship attitudes, (2) entrepreneurship abilities, and (3) entrepreneurship aspirations. These three subindexes contain micro and macro aspects of entrepreneurship. In other words, GEI is a three-component index which takes into consideration different aspects of entrepreneurial ecosystem.

GEI value for the Republic of Serbia was 30.9 in 2016. In addition to Bosnia and Herzegovina (82) and Albania (76), Serbia is the worst-ranked country in the region (74th position). In addition, it is along with the countries mentioned at the bottom of the list in Europe (in addition to Moldavia and Ukraine).

Putting in relation global entrepreneurship index and globalization index (Figure 3.7) or analysis did not show close correlation between globalization and entrepreneurship level for Serbia and countries in the region, i.e., correlation is $R^2 = 0.1173$.

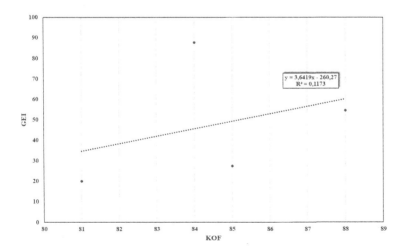

Figure 3.7 Impact of globalization on entrepreneurship development in Western Balkan countries.

Source: Radović-Marković (2018a).

Comparing Serbia to neighbor states, it is relatively well ranked in the subindex which measures the relationship toward entrepreneurship (57 position), since entrepreneurs in Serbia observe better business opportunities, are ready to take risks with no fear of failure, network more, and are innovative. According to the subindex of entrepreneurial ability, Serbia is the worst ranked (117 position), while based on the subindex, entrepreneurship intentions are among the worse ranked in the region (80 position), i.e., only Albania has worse ranking. The greatest weaknesses refer to insufficient application of new technologies, low competitiveness level, possibility to achieve better growth, and internationalization of business. In addition, the education level of new entrepreneurs is still low and there is expressed the lack of entrepreneurial experience and skills. In addition, these data point to the fact that new businesses are created more for existential necessity rather than the observed business possibilities and good business ideas.

In Serbia there is still a low level of education of new entrepreneurs and a lack of entrepreneurial experience and skills expressed. Entrepreneurship education is required at all levels of education – from elementary to high education, where through programs that promote entrepreneurship, we enable acquisition of skills and knowledge for founding and development of business. "Development of entrepreneurship talent is of an exceptional significance for maintenance of competitive advantages at global market and conditions of new economy, which is catalyzed by innovations" therefore, among the scientists, educators, and creators of economic policy, there has become more and more clear the role of a quality entrepreneurship education and its nourishment in order to develop entrepreneurial talent among the young people. Therefore, solution in the aspect of raising the competences of potential entrepreneurs should be sought through entrepreneurial education, which can contribute not only to the increase of the number of new companies but also the reduction of mistakes in business. In addition, it has a special significance in the preparation of the young to be responsible and active individuals who will choose entrepreneurial jobs for their careers. This claim is also supported by empirical studies, which confirm the thesis that education for entrepreneurship increases entrepreneurship abilities (Hatten & Ruhland, 1995; Ede et al., 1998; Hansemark, 1998).

Recent studies carried out in Serbia among the students between 20 and 25 years have pointed to the fact that the young show a certain interest for dealing with entrepreneurial activities.

To the question what is crucial for achievement of business success of entrepreneurs, the respondents have largely answered (47%) that knowledge plays a crucial role. In addition, even 80% of respondents confirm this opinion by the answer that formal entrepreneurial education is required for encouragement of entrepreneurial abilities of students. In addition, this study has also shown that students who have passed the training in entrepreneurship domain have greater entrepreneurial potential, are more motivated, and have greater self-confidence in relation to those who did not pass this type of education. As one of the main obstacles to enter entrepreneurial waters after finishing education, students see enormous tax burdens and duties, (64%), an inability to charge their receivables (17%), as well as the lack of market (11%) and inability to provide favorable loans (8%).

According to the annual report of the World Bank on business conditions for 2017. (Doing business 2017), Serbia has taken the 47th position from 190 countries. Namely, in Serbia there has significantly come to the improvement of business environment in the last couple of years, i.e., from 2014–2017 there has been an improvement by 44 places in ranking. From the countries in the region, those with better positions than Serbia are Macedonia (10) and Croatia (43). Macedonia is the best ranked, having in mind that it has performed comprehensive reforms in the domain of small and medium enterprises business. Not only have the reforms gone toward the reduction of time, elimination of duties, and reduction of procedures but also through the establishment of centralized register, complete process has been transferred from the domain of judicial power in the administration domain.

Based on a White Book (2016), in Serbia it has significantly come to the improvement of business environment in the last couple of years, i.e., from 2014–2017 it has made progress by 44 positions in ranking. Serbia has made the greatest progress in the fields of real estate and construction, protection of competition and consumers, public notary, as well as in telecommunication, oil and gas, and private insurance sectors. The least progress, according to the opinion of foreign investors, published in the White Book in 2016, was achieved in the field of taxes and labor and legal regulations, both in the aspect of laws that refer to foreign exchange business, bankruptcy, and protection of exciters, as well as in the sector of food and agriculture and maintenance means. Such a position of Serbia by entrepreneurship development criteria points to business barriers and still inadequate business climate in the country (Table 3.4).

Table 3.4 The greatest business barriers in Western Balkan countries, 2016

	Serbia	Macedonia	B&H	Albania	Montenegro
Access to financing	11.7	14.8	7.3	10.1	17.4
Tax rate	10.6	13.5	7.9	21.3	14.2
Corruption	9.0	12.6	13.0	23.6	9.4
Tax regulations	9.0	11.3	8.8	1.9	9.1
Weak labor ethics in domestic labor	8.7	10.1	3.3	5.6	9.1
Inadequately educated labor	8.1	7.1	5.3	11.3	8.1
Inadequate infrastructure	7.9	5.8	5.3	4.5	7.5
Exchange rate regime	6.9	4.5	0.6	0.4	6.2
Constraining regulations on labor	6.3	4.4	3.6	0.0	4.6
Lack of innovation capacity	5.5	4.2	2.5	0.6	3.8
Inefficient state bureaucracy	4.5	3.8	13.7	6.6	3.0
Inflation	3.7	3.6	1.4	2.4	2.9
Crime	3.7	2.2	5.0	2.4	2.4
Political instability	3.4.0	0.8	10.5	8.9	1.2
Poor public health	0.6	0.8	0.8	0.2	0.5
State instability	0.4	0.5	11.1	0.3	0.4

Source: World Economic Forum, Executive Opinion Survey 2016.

3.7 SMEs and Resilience

Organizational resilience can be defined as a sum of essential concepts. These essential concepts include enterprise risk management, governance, quality assurance, information security, business continuity, and culture and values supported by adaptive leadership. In the opinion of a number of experts on the field of resilience, "enterprise resilience is sometimes referred to as the corporate immune system" (Chesley, 2016).

Organizational resilience over the past decade has increased attention on implementing policies and programs that are based on scientific evidence. There are several areas for resilience research, in particular, the relationship between human and organizational resilience; organizational and infrastructural resilience; and how the resilience is conceived in small and medium-sized enterprises, identifying particular factors that affect organizational resistance

(Radović-Marković, 2018a). Also, should be explored the link between leader resilience and organization resilience and finally, the connection between SME resilience and the organization's geographical location (Wishart, 2018).

Researchers have different views of what constitute SME resilience. According to a number of scientists, resilience research with an SME focus is a limited field (Wishart, 2018). Namely, resilience research into small business organizations is relatively rare (Conz et al., 2017; Linnenluecke, 2017; Radović-Marković, 2017).

Policymakers and theorists in this field have proposed various models to improve the adaptive capacities of SMEs by concentrating on identification of risks and opportunities for strengthening their human and institutional capacities. "Yet understanding what makes organizations resilient in the real world is critical to thinking about developing strategies for strengthening their resilience" (Barasa et al., 2018). In the opinion of a number of experts on the field of resilience, "enterprise resilience is sometimes referred to as the corporate immune system" (Chesley, 2016).

A catastrophe can strike any organization. It can come in the form of a storm, flood, fire, terrorist actions, product contamination, or simply due to unsuccessful quality control of products (Radović-Marković, 2018a). It is therefore necessary to investigate SME behavior, as well as their coping skills and resilience in facing up to various internal and external business conditions and challenges. In line with this, there is a need for an appropriate SME resilience agenda that mitigates measures against business shocks and unexpected events. In literature, it has been recognized that the SME sector poses various government agendas (Abbott & Allen, 2005; Sexton et al. 2006; Conz et al., 2017). There is also an evidence that governments, SME associations, and supply chain companies work with the SMEs to facilitate behavioral changes so that SMEs could develop their coping measures and decision-making skills (Ingirige et al., 2008). These measures can cover a range of issues including (Broughton, 2011) the following:

- financial measures;
- helping SMEs to access new markets and to invest in research, development, and innovation;
- providing specific advice and consultancy to SMEs, usually on themes such as how to set up operations or financial advice;
- simplification of administrative procedures;
- support for job creation, which usually takes the form of providing financial incentives, such as reduced employer social

security contributions for employers hiring unemployed people;

- enabling temporary reductions in the workforce, primarily through the provision of short-time work. This measure has been used widely throughout the EU during the recent crisis;
- supporting training. Training is recognized as a key instrument in ensuring employability, not just during an economic crisis, but throughout an employee's working life. SMEs often find it difficult to release employees for training and to fund training in general;
- some very targeted sectoral measures, which are in place in some countries, in addition to measures specifically targeting entrepreneurship.

Despite the external events can provoke unanticipated consequences for businesses, such as a sudden drop in sales or resources (Linnenluecke, 2017), researchers Ayala and Manzano (2014) showed that resilience has predictive validity. In line with this, entrepreneurs that score highly for resilience characteristics are likely to run successful business that grows over time.

3.7.1 Global Index of Resilience

According to human resource management (HRM), an organization is resilient if people can respond to changes with minimum stress promptly and efficiently, and these are positive possibilities of adaptation which separate competition (Radović Marković et al., 2017).

Resilience concept is used to get an explanation how a number of countries can rapidly get out of the crisis and recover from different shocks (natural disasters, financial, and other crises) and after that reach a relatively high level of GDP per capita, while other economies are not able to do that.

Global index of resilience for 2017 included 130 countries. Among the countries of Western Balkan, the best ranked is Croatia (41), and the worst, Albania (107). Serbia has taken the best position after Croatia. All the countries analyzed in 2017 in comparison to the previous year have improved their rank by one position.

It was determined that index of resilience, constructed by Briguglio (2014), is positively correlated with GDP per capita. Our research for Balkan countries confirmed this statement. Namely, $R^2 = 0.7962$ (Figure 3.8).

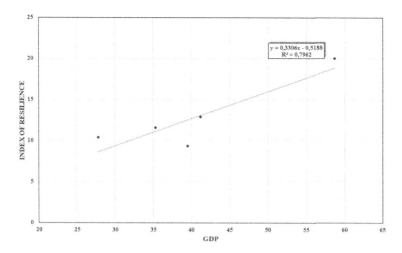

Figure 3.8 Correlation between index of resilience and GDP per capita in
        Balkan countries.
Source: Radović-Marković (2018a).

Namely, in spite of high exposure to external shocks, a great
number of small countries manage to sustain themselves in economic aspect and continue their development, having in mind their
relatively high consumption per capita. Among small countries
that have registered high resilience, there are separated the countries such as Singapore, Switzerland, and Luxembourg.

According to Briguglio's opinion (2014), Singapore and Malta
have adopted four main strategic directions, which can explain
their success and serve as a model for other small countries. These
are as follows:

a   strong regulatory framework,
b   identification and support of production niches,
c   promotion and creation of production clusters, and
d   encouragement of regional cooperation.

It is of particular importance to encourage the regional cooperation between small countries. It can lead to useful synergies, such as
training for entrepreneurship, information and knowledge exchange,
common financial institutions, and others. Such a regional grouping
would reduce efforts of doubling the jobs and institutions of some
small countries, which would enable the reduction of economic costs.

By comparing the index of globalization and global index of resilience, we can observe dependence $R^2 = 0.9726$. Namely, as the country is more globally integrated, it is more resistant to negative incentives, which come from global business environment.

Resilience of economy of a country cannot be achieved if the organizations are not also resistant to negative impacts. Therefore, many believe that resilience of a country and resilience of small and medium companies are just like two sides of one coin (Radović-Marković, 2017). By organizational resilience, we do not imply only "survival" and "existence" of the company, but also comprehensiveness in the access to business success. Therefore, organizational resilience is not a defensive strategy, but a strategy aimed to the improvement of business, which enables business leaders to take risk with a higher level of security (Allen, 2016).

Recent studies in Serbia (2016) have shown that Serbian organizations have a low resilience level. For the needs of that study, there were used qualitative methods/direct contact with respondents; in cases where it was not possible, to carry out an interview, electronic questionnaire was used. The sample consisted of 50 respondents from 40 different organizations (information sector, educational institutions, banks and financial institutions). Information sector was present with 46%, education with 38%, while financial was 16%.

In sample structure, there participated 40% women and 60% men. About 89% respondents were aged between 31 and 40 years and in the position of a team leader of an organization. For the interpretation of the data obtained, there were used methods of analysis and synthesis, as well as deduction.

In the study there were four crucial questions, which should provide an answer to the following:

1 Which external factors have had the most negative impact on the business of their organization?
2 Are there planned potential "internal and external shocks" in the organization?
3 Which are the primary internal factors which have a negative impact on the organization's business?
4 Which are the most efficient methods for encouraging the organization's resilience?

For an SME, adaptation to flood risk or other catastrophes may come via business continuity. Accordingly, understanding the way organizations are resilient in the real world is crucial for thinking about developing strategies to enhance their resilience. It has been estimated in many papers that around half of all enterprises experiencing a catastrophe and having no effective recovery plans fail within the next twelve months. To survive in business after disasters requires careful preplanning. Due to nonplanning, companies, employees, and shareholders are exposed to rather unnecessary risks. In addition to insufficient planning, companies have also shown inefficiency in the implementation of these plans. "One of the main obstacles to the successful implementation of the business continuity plan in small and medium enterprises is the lack of understanding of the importance of business continuity" (Radović-Marković, 2018b, p. 102). In addition, it is imperative to take into account that when integrating the company into global business flows, current and potential business partners will see the resilience as a key criterion of cooperation.

The study has shown that organizations in Serbia have special programs in order to raise the level and resistance to negative incentives. In addition, these questions are not in companies being dealt by especially educated people in this domain (risk managers, emergency managers). Despite that, our study has shown that only 12% of organizations stop working in case of a crisis, while 36% continue the work, holding onto the standard routines in their business (Radović-Marković, 2017, p. 37). Indicative according to the obtained results of our research is the fact that there is a large percentage of those enterprises that do nothing in conditions of disasters and major business quakes (29.51%), since they are not prepared for them and do not have a risk management strategy (Figure 3.9). Therefore, they are most often waiting for the situation to stabilize itself.

In addition, our research has shown that there is not a large percentage of small and medium-sized enterprises that have secured their assets (16.39%). However, insurance companies have the know-how, experience, and tools for risk assessment and implementation of specific interventions in order to reduce subsequent damages and losses, which can be an exceptional support to small and medium enterprises in crisis conditions. "Despite this, more than 50% of the respondents answered that they are not familiar with all the products of the insurance industry in our market" (Radović-Marković, 2018b, p. 103).

This study has also shown that the greatest threats from business environment for Serbian organizations are also big competition in the market and lack of financial funds. In case there comes to

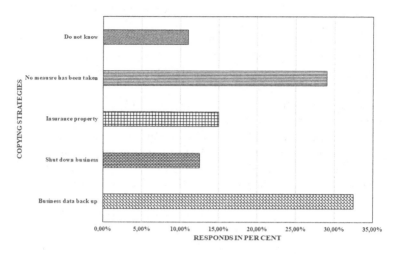

Figure 3.9 Coping strategies.
Source: Radović-Marković et al. (2017).

greater shocks and negative impacts, the first thing that is applied is data protection in the IT sector.

> Approximately 40% of respondents believe that motivation of organizations to continuously learn is the key to raise the resilience level, while 38% of them believe that flexibility of organization is important and the ability of leader to predict the business risk.
>
> (p. 38)

Therefore, leaders must evaluate in advance the endangerment level of the enterprise to understand the interdependence between business processes, information, and technologies within one organization. In addition, entrepreneurs and managers should deal with high rates of failure of small companies and pay greater attention to their liquidity, money flow, and seasonal fluctuations.

Conclusion

Results of our study have not shown a tight correlation between globalization level and entrepreneurship level, tested for Serbia and region countries. Therefore, the hypothesis H0 is not confirmed. On the other hand, the hypothesis H1 is entirely confirmed.

Also, the hypothesis H2 is entirely confirmed, having in mind that only learning organizations can make progress and reach resistance level to all negative encouragements. Those organizations that refuse to learn and improve will definitely one day become irrelevant to the industry. According to this statement, we can mention the example of Nokia. Its president used to say to his colleagues "we didn't do anything wrong, but somehow, we lost. However, they missed out on learning, they missed out on changing, and thus they lost the opportunity at hand to make it big.

The hypotheses H3 and H4 are also confirmed. Namely, our research showed that one of the main obstacles to the successful implementation of the business continuity plan in small and medium enterprises is the lack of understanding of the importance of business continuity. In addition, the analysis showed that small businesses have little awareness of the importance of insurance to encourage the resilience of SMEs.

Our research has simultaneously shown that Serbia in the last couple of years has reached improvements in implementation of internal reforms and creation of a more favorable business climate for development of small and medium companies and strengthening of the business sector. Thus, the development of entrepreneurship in the beginning of 2016 was on the list of priorities of the Government of the Republic of Serbia, which continued throughout 2017 as well. There was also established the Development Agency of Serbia (DAS), as the crucial executive institution in charge of implementation of entrepreneurship policy in the country.

Serbia should without any doubt continue in the perspective with internal reforms. In addition, having in mind that Serbia is a small country, the only way for it to achieve economic growth and become economically more relevant in the global framework is for it to a greater extent than before internationalize its business activities and start acting in international markets. That implies that Serbia should become a more serious "global player," However, the manner in which the positioning of small and medium enterprises will be done in the global market will depend on their potentials and limitations – resources available, as well as their ability to react to variable changes in the market, having in mind that all the waves of globalization in modern history were in one way or another encouraged by technical and technological innovations that have reflected itself on change of business in a fundamental manner. Namely, in accordance with these changes, enterprises look for new models of organizational relations that correspond more to the existing business environment. The examples of leading SME throughout the world point out that particularly information and communication technologies, then innovations and implementation of strategic management and risk management in small enterprises become more and more important for their survival and development. In addition, the economic resilience needs to be strengthened. For that reason, achieving economic resilience should be one of the overriding goals of the implementation of long growth-promoting government macroeconomic policies. In accordance with that, winning companies are those that rapidly respond to challenges and turn all the changes in new possibilities. Therefore, their good practice should be used and implemented in entrepreneurial sector of Serbia and Western Balkan countries.

References

Abbott, C., & Allen, S., 2005, Facilitating Innovation: The Role of the Centre For Construction Innovation. *International Journal of Strategic Property Management*, 9, pp. 79–89.

Acs, Z., Szerb, L., Autio, E., & Lloyd, A., 2017. Global Entrepreneurship Index 2017. Available at: www.researchgate.net/profile/Laszlo_Szerb2/publication/316595971_Global_Entrepreneurship_Index_2017/links/5906107ba6fdccd580d37ba1/Global-Entrepreneurship-Index-2017.pdf

AFET, 2017, Serbia's Cooperation with China, the European Union, Russia and the United States of America, Belgium.

Allen, T. (2016). Why Organisational Resilience Is the Key to Long-Term Prosperity for SMEs, BSI.

Altenburg, T., & Drachenfels, C., 2008. *Business Environment Reforms: Why It Is Necessary to Rethink Priorities and Strategies*. German Development Institute.

Atristain, C., & Rajagopal, 2010. Conceptual Perspectives on Organizational Performance and Competitiveness of SMEs in Mexico. *Journal of Transnational Management*, 15(4), pp. 322–349.

Audretsch, D., 1991. New-Firm Survival and the Technological Regime. *Review of Economics and Statistics*, 60(3), pp. 441–450.

Awuah, G. B., & Amal, M., 2011. 'Impact of Globalization: The Ability of Less Developed Countries' (LCDs') Firms to Cope with Opportunities and Challenges. *European Business Review*, 23(1), pp. 120–132.

Ayala, J. C., & Manzano, G., 2014. The Resilience of the Entrepreneur. Influence on the Success of the Business. A Longitudinal Analysis. *Journal of Economic Psychology*, 42, pp. 245–251.

Barasa, E., Mbau, R., & Gilson, L., 2018. What Is Resilience and How Can It Be Nurtured? A Systematic Review of Empirical Literature on

Organizational Resilience. *International Journal of Health Policy and Management*, x(x), pp. 1–13.

Beck, T., Demirguc-Kunt, A., & Levine, R., 2005, September. SMEs, Growth, and Poverty: Cross-Country Evidence. *Journal of Economic Growth*, 10(3), pp. 199–229.

BIRN, 2018. $3bn Economic Agreements Boost China's Role in Serbia. Available at: www.balkaninsight.com/en/article/new-agreements-boost-china-role-in-serbia-09-18-2018

Bloom, N., & Van Reenen, J., 2002. Patents, Real Options and Firm Performance. *Economic Journal*, 112(478), pp. C97–116.

Bräutigam, D., & Woolcock, M., 2001. Small States in a Global Economy, Discussion Paper No. 2001/37. www.wider.unu.edu/sites/default/files/dp2001-37.pdf [Accessed 17 July 2017].

Briguglio, L. (2014). A Revised Vulnerability and Resilience Framework. Report Commissioned by the Commonwealth Secretariat.

Broughton, A. (2011). SMEs and Their Strategies for Coping with the Recession, Institute for Employment Studies, Brighton. Available at: www.employment-studies.co.uk/news/smes-and-their-strategies-coping-recession [Accessed 15 August 2018].

Campaniaris, C, Hayes, S, Jeffrey, M., & Murray, R., 2010. The Applicability of Cluster Theory to Canada's Small and Medium Sized Apparel Companies. *Journal of Fashion Marketing and Management*, 15(1), pp. 8–26.

CDM, 2017. Crna Gora u evropskom vrhu po realnom rastu BDP-a. September 2017.

Chesley, D., 2016. How Enterprise Resilience Can Help Drive Growth in Financial Services –Enterprise Resilience – An Important Business Capability Today. Australia: Pwc. Available at: www.pwc.com.au/pdf/how-enterprise-resilience-can-help-drive-growth-in-financial-services.pdf

Chatterjee, A., & Wehrhahn, R., 2017. Insurance for Micro, Small, and Medium-Sized Enterprises, Asian Development Bank. http://hdl.handle.net/11540/7284

Conz, E., Denicolai, S., & Zucchella, A., 2017. The Resilience Strategies of SMEs in Mature Clusters. *Journal of Enterprising Communities*, 11(1), pp. 186–210.

Devinney, T., Markman, G., Pedersen, T., & Tihanyi, L., 2016. *Global Entrepreneurship: Past, Present & Future*. Bingley: Emerald Group Publishing Limited.

Dreher, A. (2006). Does Globalization Affect Growth? Empirical Evidence from a New Index. *Applied Economics*, 38(10), pp. 1091–1110.

Doing Business, 2017. World Bank. Available at: www.doingbusiness.org/content/dam/doingBusiness/media/Annual-Reports/English/DB17-Report.pdf

Ede, F. O., Panigrahi, B., & Calcich, S. E., 1998. African American Students' Attitudes Toward Entrepreneurship Education. *Journal of Education for Business*, 73(5), pp. 291–296.

European Western Balkans, 2018. Assessing Russia's Economic Footprint in the Western Balkans. Available at: https://europeanwesternbalkans. com/2018/03/08/assessing-russias-economic-footprint-western-balkans/

Eurostat, 2017. http://ec.europa.eu/eurostat/statistics-explained/images/b/ b5/Real_GDP_growth%2C_2006-2016_%28%25_change_compared_ with_the_previous_year%3B_%25_per_annum%29_YB17.png

Gemmell, N., Kneller, R., & Sanz, I., 2008. Foreign Investment, International Trade and the Size and Structure of Public Expenditures. *European Journal of Political Economy*, 24(1), pp. 151–171.

Hansemark, O. (1998). The Effects of an Entrepreneurship Programme on Need for Achievement and Locus of Control of Reinforcement. *International Journal of Entrepreneurship Behaviour and Research*, 4(1), pp. 28–50.

Hänsel, L., & Feyerabend, F. C., 2018. *The Influence of External Actors in the Western Balkans*. Bonn: Konrad-Adenauer-Stiftung.

Hatten, T., & Ruhland, 1995. Student Attitudes toward Entrepreneurship as Affected by Participation in an SBI Program. *Journal of Education for Business*, 7(4), pp. 224–227.

Helmer, C., & Rogers, M., 2008. *Innovation and the Survival of New Firms across British Regions*. Oxford.

Heng, G. M., & Wong, J., 2015. *Business continuity management implementation for small and medium sized enterprises*, BCM Institute, United Kingdom.

Iandoli, L., Quinto, I., De Liddo, A., & Shum, S. B., 2014. Socially Augmented Argumentation Tools: Rationale, Design and Evaluation of a Debate Dashboard. *International Journal of Human-Computer Studies*, 72, pp. 298–319.

Incekara, A., & Savrul, M., 2012, October 11th–13th. The Effect of Globalization on Foreign Trade and Investment in Eurasian Countries. *International Conference on Eurasian Economies*. Almaty: Kazakistan Republic, pp. 23–30.

Ingirige, B., Jones, K., & Proverbs, D., 2008. Investigating SME Resilience and their Adaptive Capacities to Extreme Weat Her Events: A Literature Review and Synthesis. Available at: www.researchgate.net/ publication/228706390_Investigating_SME_resilience_and_their_ adaptive_capacities_to_extreme_weather_events_A_literature_re- view_and_synthesis [Accessed 20 July 2018].

Klette. T. J., & Kortum, S., 2004. Innovating Firms and Aggregate Innovation. *Journal of Political Economy*, 112(5), pp. 986–1018.

Knight, G., 2000. Entrepreneurship and Marketing strategy: The SME under Globalization. *Journal of International Marketing*, 8(2), pp. 12–32.

Knight, G., 2001. Entrepreneurship and Strategy in the International SME. *Journal of International Management*, 7(3).

Kuepper, J., 2018. *Globalization: Good or Bad for Developed Countries?* International Investing. Available at: www.thebalance.com/globalization- good-or-bad-for-developed-countries-4011193

Le Corre, P., & Vuksanovic, V., 2019. Serbia: China's Open Door to the Balkans. *The Diplomat*, January 01. Available at: https://thediplomat. com/2019/01/serbia-chinas-open-door-to-the-balkans/

Lederman, D., & Lesniak, J. T., 2017. *Open and Nimble: Finding Stable Growth in Small Economies, Summary*. Washington, DC: World Bank. Available at: https://openknowledge.worldbank.org/handle/10986/26304 License: CC BY 3.0 IGO.

Lee, K., & Carter, S., 2005. *Global Marketing Management*. Oxford: Oxford University Press.

Lee, E., & Vivarelli, M., 2006. The Social Impact of Globalization in the Developing Countries. *International Labour Review*, 145(3), pp. 167–184.

Lesáková, L., 2014. Small and Medium Enterprises in the New World of Globalization. *Forum Scientiae Oeconomia*, 2(3).

Lindert, P., & Williamson, J., 2001. Does Globalization Make the World More Unequal?. www.nber.org/books/bord03-1

Linnenluecke, M. K., 2017. Resilience in Business and Management Research: A Review of Influential Publications and a Research Agenda. *International Journal of Management Reviews*, 19(1), pp. 4–30. doi:10.1111/ijmr.12076.

Međak, V., 2018. Effects of Stabilisation and Association Agreements and CEFTA2006 on WB6 European Integration and Regional Cooperation: Achievements and Ways Forward. European Movement in Serbia.

Milner, H. V., & Kubota, K., 2005. Why the Move to Free Trade? Democracy and Trade Policy in the Developing Countries. *International Organization*, 56(1), pp. 107–143.

National Bank of Serbia, 2017. Available at: www.nbs.rs/internet/english/

Petrylė, V., 2016. Does The Global Competitiveness Index Demonstrate The Resilience of Countries to Economic Crises?. *Ekonomika*, 95(3).

Pollalis, Y. A., & Dimitriou, N. K., 2008. Knowledge Management in Virtual Enterprises: A Systemic Multi-Methodology Towards the Strategic Use of Information. *International Journal of Information Management*, 28, 305–321.

Radović-Marković, M., 2017. Podsticanje rezilijentnosti preduzeća u Srbiji = Fostering Resilience of the Enterprises in Serbia. In: M. Krstić (ed.), *Proceedings*. Kruševac: College "Prof. dr Radomir Bojković", str. 1–7.

Radović-Marković, M., 2018a. *Globalization Impact on Entrepreneurship in Small Countries with Focus on Serbia and Western Balkan*. New York: Nova Science Publishers.

Radović-Marković, M., 2018b. *Enhancing Resilience of SMEs through Insurance in Serbia*. Serbia: Faculty of Economics, Belgrade University.

Radović-Marković, M., Shoaib Farooq, M., & Markovic, D., 2017. Strengthening the Resilience of Small and Medium-Sized Enterprises. In: I. Takács (ed.), *Management, Enterprise and Benchmarking in the 21st century IV: "Global Challenges, Local Answers"*. Budapest: Óbuda University, pp. 345–356. http://ebooks.ien.bg.ac.rs/1119/1/meb.pdf.

Republican Bureau of Statistics, 2017. *Latest Indicators*, Serbia. Available at: www.stat.gov.rs/en-US/aktuelni-pokazatelji

Ruzzier, M, Hisrich, R.D., & Antoncic, B., 2006. 'SME internationalization research: past, present and future', *Journal of Small Business and Enterprises Development*, 13(4), pp. 476–497.

Sadeghi, H., & Sameti, M., 2012. The Impact of Globalization on Government Size in Selected Asian Countries. *Journal of Research in Economic Development*, Second year, Sixth issue, Spring.

Sakai, K., 2002. Global Industrial Restructuring: Implications for Smaller Firms, STI Working Paper 2002/4, Paris: OECD.

Samimi, P., & Jenatabadi, H. S., 2014. Globalization and Economic Growth: Empirical Evidence on the Role of Complementarities. *PLoS One*, 9(4).

Seila, S. M., 2014. *The Impact of Globalization on the Leading Small and Medium Enterprises in Nairobi County in Kenya*, School of Business, University of Nairobi.

Sexton, M., Barrett, P., & Aouad, G., 2006. Motivating Small Construction Companies to Adopt New Technology. *Building Research and Information*, 34(1), pp. 11–22.

Skilling, D., 2012. *There is No Such Thing as Domestic Policy*. Singapore: Landfall Strategy Group Pte. Ltd.

Smolková, E., 2010. *Strategické partnerstvá ako fenomén globálnej ekonomiky*. Bratislava: Infopress.

Southwick, S. M., Bonanno, G. A., Masten, A. S., Panter-Brick, C., & Yehuda, R., 2014. Resilience Definitions, Theory, and Challenges: Interdisciplinary Perspectives. *European Journal of Psychotraumatology*, 5, 1–14. Available at: https://doi.org/10.3402/ejpt.v5.25338

Stiglitz, J., 2003. Globalization and Its Discontents. 1st ed. New Yorl: W. W. Norton & Company.

Schwab, K., 2016. *The Global Competitiveness Report, 2016–2017 to 2017–2018*. World Economic Forum.

Ursprung, H., 2006. *The Impact of Globalization on the Composition of Government Expenditures: Evidence from Panel Data*. CESifo Working, Paper No.1755.

Wishart, M., 2018. *Business Resilience in an SME Context: A Literature Review*. Enterprise Research Centre and Warwick Business School.

White Book, 2016. *Cord Magazine*, Belgrade, Serbia.

World Bank, 2000. Small States: Meeting Challenges in the Global Economy, *Pristupljeno*, 15 July 2017.

About the Authors

Mirjana Radović-Marković, PhD

She completed her education from the Faculty of Economics in Belgrade, where she got her PhD in 1987. After her completing her dissertation, she continued her advanced studies in the Netherlands, the United States, and Russia, where she specialized in 1988 at Lomonosov University in the multidisciplinary studies department.

Her scientific career started at the Economics Institute in Belgrade and continued later at the Institute of Economic Sciences, also in Belgrade. Meanwhile, she was full-time and part-time engaged as a professor in numerous universities worldwide. She teaches "Entrepreneurship" at the government University of Kragujevac (Serbia) and Faculty of Business and Entrepreneurship in Belgrade (Serbia), as well as the "Applied Business Economics and Entrepreneurship" at the Irish University Business School, London, "Female Entrepreneurship" at Akamai University, "Principles of Entrepreneurship – Applications for Genealogy Business" at the American School of Genealogy, Heraldry, and Documentary Sciences, Como, Mississippi, and "Entrepreneurship and Female Entrepreneurship" at the International College of Management and Technology (ICMT) – Center for Women and Gender Studies. In addition, she has taught worldwide classes such as "Women as Entrepreneurs" and "Global Challenge" (GVF) at the Faculty Farleigh Dickinson University, New Jersey, United States. She is an editor-in-chief of the following peer journals: *Economic Analysis*; *Women's Entrepreneurship and Education*; *Journal of Entrepreneurship and Business Resilience*; and *International Review*, which is on the Thomson Reuters list. By invitation, she has given a number of lectures abroad. She did a presentation during the meeting of OECD experts in Istanbul, Turkey (March, 2010) and gave a lecture at Said Business School (June, 2010), Oxford University United Kingdom; Franklin College, Lugano, Switzerland (2011); the Faculty of Economics, University in Miskolc, Hungary, in 2009; the University St. Kliment Ohridski, Sofia, Bulgaria (since 2012–up to now); the University of Wroclaw, Poland (2014); the Academy of Science and Arts of the Republic of Srpska (since 2014–up to now); the Montenegrin Academy of Sciences and Arts (2011, 2013, 2014, 2017); the Faculty of Economics, Podgorica, Montenegro University; etc.

Since 2009 until present she has been a head of the Center of Macroeconomic Research of Institute of Economic Sciences, Belgrade. In addition, she is the head of the research and development center, Faculty of Business Economics and Entrepreneurship, Belgrade.

In October 2016 she was elected to the National Council for Science, the Republic of Serbia, which alone represents economic sciences in the country. Before her election to the National Council for Science, from 2010 to 2016 she was a member of the Committee for Social Sciences, Ministry of Science and Education, Republic of Serbia.

In October 2017 she was awarded the Tomislav Popovic award "for outstanding contribution in science" by the Institute of Economic Sciences where she has been employed since 2004. In March 28 she was awarded the Kapetan Misa Anastasijevic award for the highest contribution in science and entrepreneurship promotion by the University of Belgrade and the University of Novi Sad, Serbia.

She is an elected member of the Academia Europea (EA), London, United Kingdom (2012), and a member of the Committee on Economic and Management of the Academia Europea (EA), the Royal Society of the Arts in the United Kingdom (the RSA), World Academy of Arts and Sciences, United States, and the Royal Economic Society, United Kingdom.

Published books by Routledge:

1   Mirjana Radović-Marković and Beatrice Avolio Allechi (2013), *Women and Entrepreneurship Female Durability, Persistence and Intuition at Work*, Ashgate –Routledge, Great Britain, September 2013, ISBN: 978-1-4094–6618-5.
2   Mirjana Radović-Marković and Beatrice Avolio Allechi, (2017), *Qualitative Methods in Economics*, Routledge, United Kingdom.

Rajko Tomaš, PhD

Professor Rajko Tomaš earned his summa cum laude undergraduate degree in Economics from the Faculty of Economics at the University of Banja Luka in 1979. In 1982, he earned his summa cum laude MPhil in the field of theoretical economics at the Faculty of Economics, University of Belgrade. He obtained his PhD from the Faculty of Economics, University of Belgrade, in 1988. As a British Council scholarship holder, he was educated in the United Kingdom (BS Norwich) in 1998/99. In 2003, he had a study visit to Ireland (Irish Tax and Customs). He speaks English and Russian fluently.

Within years spent in scientific research, his main areas of interest have been focused around the laws of the market economy, market institutions, macroeconomic and microeconomic equilibrium, transition to the market economy, sectoral economic policies (especially the banking and tax system), economic integration, and externalities solutions and methods of economic analysis.

He teaches at the Faculty of Economics, University of Banja Luka, the following courses: Microeconomics, The Macroeconomics of Open Economies, Economic Analysis, and Economics of the Public Sector. Additionally, he was a visiting lecturer at a number of universities, a member of scientific committees of both international and local academic conferences, a member of editorial staff of a number of academic journals, and a reviewer of a vast number of academic works. He was the editor-in-chief and one of the founders of the journal *Acta Economica*. He is a member of the Editorial Board of the International Review, which is on the Thomson Reuters list. He is an editor of the Economic Editorial Board of Encyclopedia of Republic of Srpska. Professor Tomaš is a member of the Academy of Sciences and Arts of Republic of Srpska and president of its Committee for Economic Sciences.

For almost twenty years he worked as a consultant on the projects of institutions such as The World Bank Washington, UNDP, PricewaterhouseCoopers (PwC) Washington, Barents Group Washington, BearingPoint Washington and Deloitte Washington. He took significant consulting and advisory positions on the projects Macroeconomic Technical Assistance Project, Tax Administration Modernization Project, Tax Activity Project, and Tax and Fiscal Project. Working in teams of international experts, he gained an enlightened understanding of global tendencies and practical experience, applicable in capacity building and the enhancement of institutional activities. He was a member of the Standing Committee on Economic Affairs UNDP (1996–1998); Expert team of the Central Bank of Bosnia and Herzegovina; Council of the University of Banja Luka; The Council for the Science of the Republic of Srpska. He presided over the economic part of the international conference "Ten Years of Dayton and Beyond", held in Geneva on October 20 and 21, 2005. He was an economic advisor to the President of the Republic of Srpska. He worked as an advisor to the International Advisory Group for Macroeconomics Reforms (1999–2001).

He is the author of 9 books and coauthor of 11 books and has published a large number of scientific and professional papers in journals and book collections in the country and abroad. He has published a number of papers at national and international academic conferences. He participated in the realization of a number of projects, as a manager or a member of the team. He was a member of the European Economic Association (Milan), the International Fiscal Association (International Fiscal Association, Rotterdam), and the Serbian Fiscal Society (Belgrade).

His renowned pieces of work were *Microeconomic Analysis* (2016), *Crisis and Grey Economy in Bosnia and Herzegovina* (2010), *Economy of the Captured Resources* (2008), and *Fear of Entrepreneurship* (1993).

Index

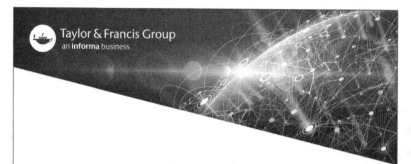

Printed in the United States
by Baker & Taylor Publisher Services